MW01035541

Carol L. Marak

SOLO AND SMART

A Roadmap for a Supportive and Secure Future

DEDICATION

Caregiving was my wake-up call and teacher. Helping my parents showed me what happens as people age. The needs older adults have aren't simple. Sometimes, they're downright terrifying. What's amazing is how varied the requirements are. From physical and mental health to personal care, handling finances, transportation, companionship, running errands, scheduling, treatments, and conversations with doctors. The needs never let up, only expand and grow until we exit this life.

May this roadmap guide souls, single and married, who are in search of support, connection, good health, purpose, God's guidance, and to have a better tomorrow. My hope is that you find confidence and certainty as the future unfolds.

1 Corinthians 10:31

SOLO AND SMART

CONTENTS

PREFACE

Caring for my parents was a wake-up call, I wondered, "Who will help care for me when older?" The struggles my parents faced were warning signs of what to expect. Divorced and childless, I lived alone in the suburbs with little savings. Caring for mom and dad required a massive effort involving three siblings and professionals. That care could someday be needed for me—only I would not have family to step up.

After my parents died, I took action to avoid the holy hell that I imagined would be my fate. SOLO AND SMART reveals a step-by-step strategy for creating a more golden future, inspiring readers to take action, to plan for their health, wealth, and more—and giving them hope. Readers will learn they aren't entirely at the mercy of what inevitably befalls most elders and that they can exercise some control over their future.

SOLO AND SMART teaches readers an easy, surefire method to assess, discover, and plan—giving them full control over how they want to live in the years ahead. You will identify and evaluate your current challenges and then build the skills and confidence to get ahead of the landmines. Readers learn how to age and live well—by shaping a future they want rather than reacting to it.

CHAPTER 1.
SMART PLANNING

The complexities of our world today call for a different way of thinking. To quote Einstein, "We can't solve problems by using the same kind of thinking when we created them." It's why following a structured blueprint is of value: It forces deep thinking, explains where the user needs to go, and helps them stay on track. Successful people have roadmaps, whether they know it or not. That's because they have a clear purpose that aligns the daily grind with the long-term aims.

When reading the book and thinking about the future: solving the potential obstacles with viable solutions, forecast three to five years out because closer than that, readers will over or underestimate the length of time it takes to make changes. And when things don't happen fast enough, people become frustrated and give up. It took 7 years for me to implement a plan that boosts security and comfort.

Rather than haphazardly spending resources on what may or may not work, the roadmap will clarify the challenges and the weaknesses that have the greatest impact on what lies ahead. It directs a reader to favorable options by way of exploring narrow concerns. The issue explored could be on having enough money, or having better health, or deciding where to live. Solo and Smart is a reader's chance to pull all the data together. After applying the smart assessment, she will have a clear sense of what's ahead—the problems she faces and the by-products of them. Once understood, the fallout and its effects on the future—the greater the chance for creating a secure lifestyle.

Consider this process a "living document" and use it regularly to record the completed activities and to reflect any changes. When evaluating the top concerns, first identify the issue and gather information. Ultimately, obtain as much data as possible. Start with the current situation and circumstances, and then determine when you want to accomplish.

Why a Plan is Needed

Most individuals focus on immediate concerns and problems. Planning forces a person to look forward and to revise and extend timeframes when the situations alter and shift. Planning's protective purpose is to minimize risk by reducing uncertainties. Just as a pilot cannot set a course once and forget about it, an individual cannot establish a goal and let the matter rest. The future is seldom certain and the further into the future, the results of a decision becomes less certain.

Factors that Make Planning Effective

Very few people are experts at managing their finances, planning retirement, building wealth, and ensuring a secure future. Effective planning is often perceived as: too hard to do, not immediately important, something to be tackled next year, and too expensive if hiring professionals.

In fact, studies show that less than 30% of Americans have a long-term plan. However, effective planning is important and it can be simple — if you know the immediate concerns and how to avoid their risks. Boiled down, it's having a clear vision of where you want to be and why. The factors of effective planning:

- A good understanding of the skills you need to attain the goals.
- A clear idea of the standard you need to achieve, and how different that is from the current one.

- A level of priority for each problem and challenge.

Steps in effective planning

The smart assessment reveals insights into the issues to address, solve, and find remedies for.

1. Define objectives. The most crucial step—determine what you want to accomplish.
2. Develop assumptions by making forecasts about the future.
3. Evaluate alternatives, options, and solutions.
4. Identify resources.
5. Plan what's next, and implement the tasks to accomplish.
6. Track changes and reevaluate your methods.

I discuss effective planning at this juncture so that readers have a sense of where the book will lead them. It's not necessary to begin the planning process at this time or to do any of the exercises in Chapter 1. Its meant to show readers where they'll end up. Once you've completed the smart assessment and smart action chapters, you're equipped with ample data for completing the exercises. Get a feel for them and keep them in mind as you read further. But at the end of the book, circle back because you will know a lot more about your current circumstances which prepares you to make a plan.

Exercise: Write a short essay about the future, combining the factors and ideas you uncovered in the assessment and the research. Write it from the perspective of someone living in the year you've selected for the outcome. Describe the world, lifestyle, domain in which the solution has emerged. Think of it as a newspaper article. It's your chance to see the future YOU.

Use these questions to brainstorm possibilities:

- What would it take to create change for this issue or problem?
- What specific skills, knowledge, and competencies do I possess?
- What areas do I need to strengthen where I am now?
- What areas do I need to strengthen for future assignments?
- What could happen that would enable me to be fully engaged and energized about an issue?
- What's the possibility here and who cares? (Rather than—What's wrong here and who is responsible?)
- What needs my immediate attention going forward?
- If success was guaranteed, what bold steps would I choose?
- What challenges might come up and how can I meet them?

- What am I not seeing?
- If I wanted to make a change, what would it be?

Personal Development Plan

- Be clear on the goal. To reduce overwhelm and to focus on action, work one goal at a time.
- Be specific.
- Know WHY you want it.
- Visualize it.
- Identify support.
- Confirm commitment.
- Set the first step.
- Set aside regular planning time.

Use this diagram to determine your objectives.

Let's Create Your Future!

Select a Situation or Issue

Relocate | Downsizing | Social Support | Connections | Health | Stay

Describe situation after change

Move to a 55+ community | Go to Italy | Save $200/mo | Lose 25 lbs

Describe what you want to change

Less debt | rightsize | lower blood pressure | be less more flexible

What do you want?

Travel | Walk 2 miles/day | Go out w/ friends | Find a job | Live in mild climate | Affordable lifestyle

Why do you want a change?

High maintenance on big house | No social circle | Low energy | Little support & few to rely on

List the Milestones or Dates to Accomplish a Goal

Use the chart below to set your milestones whether it's a timeline, goals broken down by steps, whatever your concern or issue, this graph helps you visually project the timetable for achieving goals.

List as Milestones or Dates to Accomplish

This is not set in stone—be flexible and open

To confront the risks successfully, learn which actions have the greatest impact—not just on today, but on the years ahead as conditions evolve. It's all too easy for actions that seem instinctively correct to lead us to far greater crises down the road.

CHAPTER 2:
SMART RELIANCE

Having no one to look after us in older age is a red flag for people living alone. It signals the need to prepare for the rocky years ahead. I knew if I could logically think through the hurdles of aging alone, then it might be possible to balance the risks with prevention and protection. The struggle I faced: How to unpack the systems of a poorly equipped position and replace it with competency—to become a person capable of taking care of herself when depending on family is limited?

Adult children offers a vulnerable person a second set of eyes. Boiled down, caregivers offer advocacy—to make sure the wishes of a loved one is honored. But again, because that person at risk has a son or daughter does not guarantee the family member is reliable. That's the reason older adults must become their own advocates, and it's especially important when living alone. Like me, you need to figure out who will be there for you. And like me, you might have uncovered that person to be yourself.

Self-reliance is the foundation of advocacy. When strong, it gives courage and backbone to stand up and look out for ourselves. The realization, Who will look out for me when I'm old, persistenly agitated me. That's when I learned everything I could about self-care and the influences of aging well. Doing so helped me make better choices and to take responsibility of the future. That, my friends, is self-reliance—

our pot of gold. When possessed, the person bypasses dependency on others, gains the ability to solve problems and make decisions, and be capable of caring for themselves.

To gain these skills, a person must know their strengths and weaknesses and to become resourceful through observation, inquiry, and information. Then use the knowledge to look for solutions and to ask for assistance. Self advocacy is needed most during times when you are medically evaluated and treated, filing a complaint, and developing a care plan.

Self Advocacy in Older Age

Standing up for older relatives puts caregivers in the position to advocate for themselves. The problems my sisters and I dealt with on the behalf of our parents are no different than the ones most adults will face. Aging concerns will not change. Some of us may be healthier than our relatives, or somehow be better prepared, or perhaps have saved more money, but our worries and concerns will be the same.

To create a work around for better health and well being, develop a wide-reaching interest in your life, and gain control over what happens to you. Older persons with chronic illnesses, failing health, fewer connections, and minimal resources have a higher demand to study their needs and to find options. If short in self-advocacy skills, learn them now. To transition from older adulthood to elderhood, learn the best choices for self-support and the available services that will assist.

Through family caregiving, I learned that successful advocacy increases the quality of care one receives. Neither of my parents embraced self-advocacy. My sisters and I were their voices. We'd ask the questions, request the resources, and confront the system if their needs were ignored or had fallen through the cracks. Advocacy requires communication. Having them will knock down barriers and lay the ground for unwavering independence. Patient advocates and care managers offer useful instruction on self- advocacy. They have learned the ropes to healthy aging and well-being through their work. Watching other people successfully advocate is a teaching tool. There are local organizations dedicated to teaching these skills. One in particular is MedicalHomeportal.org.

My sisters and I learned the hard way when looking out for an older person. Sometimes we were thrown out of offices and told never to come back. My sister was asked to leave the nursing home where my dad lived and to never return, and I was accused of wanting to kill my father because I requested palliative care using prescription morphine during his last days. Through the years, we hired elder law attorneys and other professionals for assistance.

A few skills we developed: Share with the doctor the medical history, current symptoms, lifestyle, and self-care. They don't have a lot of time so be brief. Prepare ahead of time. Know your family medical history: Parents | Grandparents | Siblings. Write out the questions you have about the health condition(s) and how it will affect work, home life, safety, independence, recreation, and social life before a doctor's visit. Follow up with referrals and communicating with the medical and insurance providers.

Guidelines that my mother's doctor recommended: Manage diet and weight control, exercise and recreation, stick to the prescribed medication dosage and treatment, limit alcohol, and seek help when feeling angry, lonely, or sad for long periods. Know your physical and mental health needs and inform the medical team before a serious crisis. Learn when you need emergency care: when to consult with the doctor, what hospital to report to, and the care you want. Have transportation options ready to summon and a bag packed with necessary items including medications.

For readers who do not have children, getting support requires an extra layer of planning. When there's a need to navigate the complex healthcare system, hire a patient advocate. They have the knowledge and skills to effectively communicate with medical providers. Other times include: to serve as a local emergency contact and point person —organizing medical records, medications, advance directives and building a support system.

The Road to Self-Advocacy

People who self-advocate are more likely to thrive. These skills can be learned at any age. Widows experience the need in the early stages of a partner's death. A few of my friends have lost their husbands and wives after being married for over 50 years. Most couples are joined at the hip, leaving the surviving partner in high demand of these abilities.

My dad lived four years beyond his wife. I saw the toll it took on him. Even though he was the breadwinner, he depended on my mom to handle the bills, plan and cook meals, and take care of other household duties. She was his companion for 63 years. He had just turned 85 when she died.

Similar stories from members of a Facebook group:

"I joined the Elder Orphan group several years ago, knowing this day would come, but I still had a spouse. He died last week, so I am officially an elder orphan. No kids. Absolutely no relatives—only second cousins out of state. I want to muddle through and still have a happy, healthy life, but it's going to be hard. We were joined at the hip for 43 years. I'm not 100% sure who I am now that I'm on my own. And what's especially sad is that I know very little about running a household. My husband found it easier to just do things himself than to teach me. I've lined up some handymen and joined Geek Squad. I have a very helpful financial advisor. But I'm book smart, but not street smart....and now I am going to pay the price." E.L. The Elder Orphan Facebook Group

To readers who feel like E.L., I say, "Don't invalidate yourselves. Some things are easy to figure out. You are street smart. Reaching out to professionals and services when in need is very wise. Continue to know your shortfalls and take steps that empower you. These contribute to feeling strong, confident, and independent."

Let go of perfection and the pressure of getting it right. Make sure you have a good financial advisor and tax accountant. Get recommendations and references before doing business with servce professionals. Find something meaningful to do. Consider taking a class on home repairs. Learn to research on and offline. Don't rush to make new friends. Once you enjoy your own company, they'll come. Take it slow. Take your time. Learn to sit with and accept grief, fear, uncertainty, and challenges. Place one foot in front of the other till you feel stable and balanced. Then learn where your heart wants to run. Take pride in what you can do yourself - YouTube is a useful tool for learning "how-to" skills. Faith communities are Godsends. Volunteer for a cause you believe in. Read and think deeply. Keep a journal. Pray each day. Ask God for guidance. Be kind to yourself. Trust your gut.

Self-Advocacy and Self-Confidence Practices

A life coach taught me to gain social confidence. She said that feeling anxious isn't the problem, avoiding social interactions is. Eliminate avoidance and you will overcome anxiety and the more you get out there, the closer you'll feel to others.

The processes she taught:

- Make eye contact when talking to someone. Project your voice clearly and effectively.

- Participate in small talk in the checkout line and to strangers at restaurants, coffee shops, stores, events, and the gym. Approach people who are open to you through eye contact and friendly smiles. Talk to them. You're not expected to please everyone. Take risks and meet new people.

- Try new things: Join a club, acting or an improv class, lifelong learning class. Pick up a new project, or learn a new skill. Get out of your comfort zone. Develop confidence and don't allow anxiety, fear of failure, fear of rejection, or fear of humiliation get in your way. By practicing new activities, you are confronting your fear of the unknown.

- Remain fully present and pay attention to the conversation and the cues. With practice, you will improve the social skills, ultimately making you feel more confident.

- Find support. Self-reliance means stability and confidence no matter what. Be true to self; capable of independent thought, to know one's preferences and live accordingly without worry of opinions.

In his work, Ralph Waldo Emerson believes society can negatively impact our growth. Emerson argues that self-reliance, self-trust, and individualism are ways to avoid the conformity imposed upon us. In his essay, Self-Reliance means to rely on yourself when no one is around because you are fully capable of handling a worrisome situation.

Be Your Best Friend

Become your own best friend. Understand and learn what a best friend means to you. For me, it is someone I trust with my darkest and deepest secrets and be the kind of friend I am to others; someone who will laugh at my jokes, celebrate my wins, and cry with me when I lose. A person who listens when I have troubles or when I'm down.

What is a best friend is to you? What do you hope to receive from a best friend? Write your answers: 1) What do I like about myself? What would I tell my 90 year old self? 2) Think about the people you appreciate and answer, Why am I grateful for them? What would they say about me at my wake? What would I hope they say?

Build Self-acceptance

Do two or more of these activities each week for three weeks minimum. Take notes.

Boost confidence: In a journal, list the things you are good at doing and the things that need improvement. Discuss your list with a friend or accountability partner — they can add to the list. Celebrate and develop your strengths and find ways to improve where you fall short. If you see mistakes, remind yourself that they're learning opportunities. Accept compliments and compliment yourself. When you receive a compliment, thank them and ask for details; what exactly do they like?

Recognize your own achievements and celebrate them with reward and sharing with friends.

Tools for Strength

In the Journal of Aging Research (2018), through hundreds of interviews with older adults, the researchers devised simple strategies to develop self-reliance and independence. The study laid out the useful tools:

- Keep moving. Walking is the most prevalent mode of physical activity. Good physical functioning helps maintain independence. Staying active is connected to work—it adds to good physical health.

- Remain free from debilitating illness, the very reason for managing the ones we have. And finally, develop healthy eating habits like the Mediterranean diets. Find one that consists mainly of vegetables, fruit, and grains.

- Build self-reliance and stay mentally alert: Read newspapers and books, watch TV (but not too much,) listen to the radio, eat fruit and nuts, stay active, and play games that enhance mental health. Learn new skills, handcrafts, and simple maintenance tasks.

Build a family of choice

Create a family of choice—the most viable option for solo agers with few blood relatives. Cultivating a family is significant when navigating the future alone. Having a handful of close friends helps alleviate loneliness and isolation, and being alone in the world. This group is family. Build your own core unit of friends who care about you.

Self-care goes beyond paying attention to, resolving any issues, and managing emotional, mental, and physical well-being. It stretches deep into personal understanding and finding our place in the world. The things that drive us to enjoy life. Self-care stretches beyond ourselves and pulls in other individuals we choose to love and care about.

Self-advocacy improves self-esteem, opens the door for creative problem solving, and creates a deeper sense of belonging. These skills, along with understanding the personal risks and challenges that compromise aging well, puts readers in the drivers seat of certainty.

CHAPTER 3.
SMART ROADMAP

Having a roadmap to set the direction of one's life is similar to using a map when driving. Developing a feel for the land, a mental map for aging well, is perplexing if you've never cared for another. Experienced caregivers have little trouble sensing the issues; operating as extensions of the healthcare systems, performing complex medical tasks, and ensuring a recipient's care plan adherence. Caregivers become home-based care coordinators and personal advocates— exposing them to experiences they will encounter and ultimately, learn what's needed for their own care.

When in unfamiliar territory, use a navigation system to negotiate health, where to live, find a ride, build a support network and more. The findings are based on personal assessments, such as to make a move or to rightsize, or to manage a complicated chronic illness. Having a mental map of what's ahead helps a caregiver or an older individual to analyze the current landscape.

A Personal GPS

Following a route that directs turns, avoids dead ends, and navigates detours is critical when thinking about what's ahead. Family caregiving was my Waze app. It's like having a 1:1 position guide—a set of steps or map if you will. Think how much faster you could progress and how much more time is saved from receiving feedback, helping one identify precisely where they are. Perhaps an issue becomes increasingly coherent, or shows something that has never been exposed. You are the captain of the plan, so if goals change, how to tweak them is up to you.

Kick start a personal GPS:

Anticipate the needs in advance by evaluating the challenges. Look at the issues your friends and siblings (and older relatives) have coped with then put yourself in their shoes. It's your chance to create various scenarios and consider how you would tackle or resolve. But it requires time, patience, and research. Applying due diligence unlocks additional options never before seen.

This roadmap was developed for my own long-term strategy. Health and fitness, home and location, social relationships, nearby support, faith and spiritual practices, purpose, finances and legal matters, and transportation, would be the lion's share of struggles. If health is compromised, it affects everything else. How much money one has affects where she lives, who the neighbors are, and how close to health clubs and medical facilities she is. When these work in sync, they have a sizable influence over feeling settled, stable and content.

It remains a surprise that so much emphasis is put on finances when planning for retirement. I'm not saying money isn't important, but after helping my parents, it makes more sense to take a wider-spread approach.

Life Domain Functioning

- Physical/Medical
- Family
- Employment
- Social Functioning
- Recreational
- Intellectual/Cognitive
- Living Skills
- Residential Stability
- Legal Matters
- Financial Stability
- Sleep
- Self Care
- Decision Making
- Involvement in Recovery
- Transportation
- Medication Involvement

Aging Strengths

- Family
- Social Connections
  Optimism

- Talents/Interests
  Educational
- Volunteering
- Job Spiritual/Religious
  Community
- Connectedness
- Natural Supports
- Resiliency
- Resourcefulness

Behavioral Changes

- Depression
- Anxiety
- Interpersonal Problems
- Antisocial Behavior
- Adjustment to Trauma
- Anger Control
- Substance Use
- Eating Disturbance

A nod to Laura Carstensen, Professor, Stanford University and Executive Director, Stanford Center on Longevity: Carstensen encourages all adults to take better care of their future selves and less so of their immediate gratifications—like spending too much time thinking how to feel happy this evening. Carstensen maintains the belief that the small choices people make on a daily basis exert far more influence over their health and well-being than their own genes. Yet most individuals are insensitive to patterns that put them at risk, like spending a little more money than they earn, eating poorly, disengaging from neighbors and close friends. To make matters worse, people can't comprehend the distant future.

A Roadmap

Nearly one-third of adults 55 and older are single. Even AARP reports that the largest segment of the American population is the single adult while nuclear families fall second. Solo aging doesn't necessarily mean single! And solo living shouldn't translate to having no one to count on.

Once we reach a certain age, the risks become the focus. But thinking about it is depressing because we fear we'll be lonely and alone, suffer the loss of those we love, unable to participate or to drive, and fear dependence and insecurity.

- When older, health may decline—How do I know the probability of my health years from now?

- How do I create a sense of being cared for, like the kind most family members have for one another?
- Who will watch out for me and who will meet my basic needs for companionship, friendship, and community?
- How can I know that money will outlast me?
- Is the place I live affordable, can I keep up with the maintenance, and will my monthly budget keep up with the expenses?
- What are my options? Is there a process to follow that guides me through the long-term?

Life revolves around ten domain factors. Which one(s) make you feel confident or apprehensive?

© 2021

Find Your Sweet Spot

The Roadmap assessment will assist readers to discover what's uniquely right for them—their sweet spot. It's a place of contentment—where the things you love meet your needs and preferences. Finding sweet spots is often a long process, peppered with detours and disappointments, but it is worthwhile in the end. When sweet spots are found, our whole selves, our communities and the entire world, are better for it. Here's how I found mine: I asked WHAT do I want? And then, WHY do I want it? Sweet spots lie between—the optimal place for obtaining a desirable result. WHAT: engagement and connection, WHY: I felt isolated and lonely. Sweet spot: Urban lifestyle—it resolved my isolation and loneliness because I feel connected here.

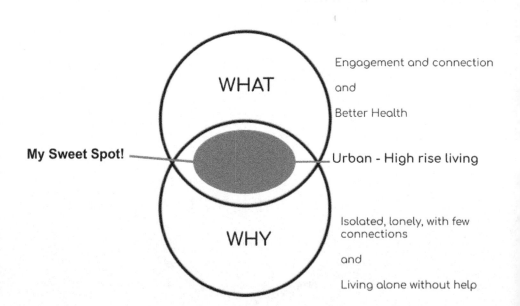

CHAPTER 4.
SMART ASSESSMENT

Let's get started! Have a notebook and pen handy. Then begin the Roadmap for a Supportive and Secure Future© assessment process.

Appraising my own top concerns, health was number one. If health was compromised, nothing mattered much. Other things would matter more; medical treatments and prescriptions, hospital stays, doctor visits, and other costly health related items. The expenses would play havoc on savings, inability to work, having a sense of purpose, and lessening the desire to engage.

HEALTH | FITNESS

Using the circle at the end of Chapter 2, self-appraise each area of the top aging issues. Let's start with Health and Fitness and proceed to the other nine. Give each question in each domain sequence an honest value ranging from 1—10, with 1 being a "difficulty or complete dilemma" and 10 is "wow, this feels good." Track your answer on a separate sheet of paper or record it digitally. When you've completed each domain sequence, tally the final result and mark it on the circle.

In this section evaluate your health and fitness by answering: How satisfied am I with..?

1. Knowledge about my family medical history? (1-10, record it)
2. Annual blood test results and screenings? (1-10, record it)

3. Daily nutrition and whole foods intake? (1-10, record it)

4. My self care routines? (1-10, record it)

5. The way you feel about yourself (1-10, record it)

6. My weight? (1-10, record it)

7. Blood pressure? (1-10, record it)

8. Blood sugar levels? (1-10, record it)

9. Cholesterol numbers? (1-10, record it)

10. Number of chronic diseases? (1-10, record it)

11. Hydration? Am I drinking enough water? (1-10, record it)

12. Activity—time spent moving? (1-10, record it)

13. Exercise and stretching program? (1-10, record it)

14. Fall Risk and Fracture risk—results of a DEXA scan? (1-10, record it)

15. General mood? (1-10, record it)

16. Time spent outside and enjoying the fresh air? (1-10, record it)

17. Energy level? (1-10, record it)

18. Nutrition and whole foods intake? (1-10, record it)

19. Am I eating enough vegetables and fruit? (1-10, record it)

20. Alcohol intake? (1-10, record it)

21. Sleep patterns? Hours spent sleeping? (1-10, record it)

22. My doctor? (1-10, record it)

23. My health insurance? (1-10, record it)

24. Functional ability? (1-10, record it)

25. Sense of well-being? (1-10, record it)

Tally the final result by adding each value within the Health | Fitness sequence, divide by 25 = _____. Record the final result on the circle labeled Health | Fitness.

DISCLAIMER: Talk with your physician before making any changes to your diet, exercise program, or altering any part of health. This tool is for self-assessing your level of satisfaction with the current health status. It is not meant nor should you use it to replace or modify any recommendations from your medical team.

HOUSING | LOCATION

In this section evaluate your housing and location by answering: How satisfied am I with..?

1. Lifestyle I live and the conditions? (1-10, record it)
2. My choice of location?
3. Its affordability? (1-10, record it)
4. Consumption of the monthly budget for my home, including maintenance and upkeep? (1-10, record it)
5. Proximity to family and friends? (1-10, record it)
6. Proximity to doctors, pharmacies, other medical facilities, shopping, senior centers, religious facilities and public libraries? (1-10, record it)
7. Ability to shop without the car? (1-10, record it)

8. The in-home support services to meet my health and social needs? (1-10, record it)

9. The crime rate of the area? (1-10, record it)

10. The area's climate?

11. My home's age-friendliness? The ability for the home and location features to meet my changing health challenges? (1-10, record it)

12. Is my home the safest place for me? (1-10, record it)

13. Caring and supportive nature where you live? (1-10, record it)

14. My eligibility for public funded or subsidized housing? (1-10, record it)

15. Proximity to certain schools or colleges? a job? to public transportation? (1-10, record it)

16. The size of the house? (1-10, record it)

17. Size of the town or city? (1-10, record it)

18. Diverse array of restaurants? (1-10, record it)

19. Landscaping and its need for care? (1-10, record it)

20. Available amenities nearby? (1-10, record it)

21. Proximity to museums and theaters, music venues, professional sports teams? (1-10, record it)

22. Ample space for outdoor activities and gardens? (1-10, record it)

23. Job opportunities? (1-10, record it)

24. Robust public transit? (1-10, record it)

25. Distance from an airport? (1-10, record it)

Tally the final result by adding each value within the Housing | Location sequence, divide by 25 = _____. Record the final result on the circle labeled Housing | Location.

FAMILY | FRIENDS | CONNECTIONS

In this section evaluate your family | friends by answering: How satisfied am I with..?

1. Daily social interactions? (1-10, record it)

2. Making new friends easily? (1-10, record it)

3. Enjoyable activities I am involved in? (1-10, record it)

4. Giving support to others? (1-10, record it)

5. The sense of inclusion to offset loneliness? (1-10, record it)

6. The emotional connections I have with friends? (1-10, record it)

7. My sense of community? (1-10, record it)

8. My pet ownership? (if applicable) (1-10, record it)

9. My ability to socially integrate? (1-10, record it)

10. The size of my social network? (1-10, record it)

11. Trust and reliability of my social network? (1-10, record it)

12. The time I listen to and talk with others? (1-10, record it)

13. The deep connections I have with friends? (1-10, record it)

14. Reciprocity of support in my friendships? (1-10, record it)

15. The encouragement I receive from and offer to friends? (1-10, record it)

16. The types of activities and engagements there are? (1-10, record it)

17. How good my friends make me feel about myself? (1-10, record it)

18. The support my friends offer during the hard times? (1-10, record it)

19. The positive mindset and the level of possibility thinking of my friends? (1-10, record it)

20. The help and support friends offer without guilt or obligation? (1-10, record it)

21. The reciprocity in my friendships? (1-10, record it)

22. The number of friends I rely on? (1-10, record it)

23. Enjoyment of doing things with close relationships? (1-10, record it)

24. Confidence to count on my neighbors for help? (1-10, record it)

25. Trusting my sense of people? (1-10, record it)

Tally the final result by adding each value within the Family | Friends sequence, divide by 25 = _____. Record the final result on the circle labeled Family | Friends.

SUPPORT COMMUNITY

In this section evaluate your Support Community by answering: How satisfied am I with..?

1. Asking others for help? (1-10, record it)
2. Others' willingness to support me when I need assistance? (1-10, record it)
3. The strength of my support community? (1-10, record it)
4. Available support groups I can connect with? (1-10, record it)
5. The number of supportive peers living nearby? (1-10, record it)
6. My willingness to help others? (1-10, record it)
7. My availability for other people and neighbors? (1-10, record it)
8. The comfortableness and openness to connect with peers? (1-10, record it)
9. The time I volunteer at church/faith/community organizations? (1-10, record it)
10. The number of people to call and invite to go on a trip for a day, have lunch out, or go to the movies? (1-10, record it)
11. Safety check-in calls or visits from neighbors? (1-10, record it)
12. The available peers who will listen to my private worries and fears? (1-10, record it)
13. People in my support network and spending time together? (1-10, record it)

14. The ease of finding someone to help me with daily chores, if sick? (1-10, record it)

15. The number of people who would check on me or bring food, if ill? (1-10, record it)

16. Available friends to drive me to the doctor's office, if unable? (1-10, record it)

17. If I had an emergency, do I know someone to call for assistance? (1-10, record it)

18. When I need suggestions on how to deal with a personal problem, do I know someone to turn to? (1-10, record it)

19. The number of invitations I receive to do things with others? (1-10, record it)

20. If I had to go out of town for a few weeks, the ease of finding someone who would look after the house or apartment (the plants, pets, garden, etc?) (1-10, record it)

21. If stranded 10 miles from home, I know a few I could call on to pick me up? (1-10, record it)

22. The effectiveness of my support network—sees my perspective and understands my feelings? (1-10, record it)

23. Enjoy open communications? (1-10, record it)

24. Feeling appreciated? (1-10, record it)

25. The time we spend together? (1-10, record it)

Tally the final result by adding each value within the Support Community sequence, divide by 25 = _____. Record the final result on the circle labeled Support Community.

LIFE PURPOSE

In this section evaluate your Life Purpose by answering: How satisfied am I with..?

1. My strong sense of personal drive and commitment? (1-10, record it)
2. My life's purpose? (1-10, record it)
3. Taking responsibility and avoiding victimhood? (1-10, record it)
4. Awareness of what inspires and energizes me? (1-10, record it)
5. Meaningfulness of life? (1-10, record it)
6. The direction I'm headed? (1-10, record it)
7. The enjoyment that my purpose gives me? (1-10, record it)
8. The sense of my purpose? (1-10, record it)
9. The way I'll be remembered after I'm gone? (1-10, record it)
10. Plans for the future—do they match my true interests and desires? (1-10, record it)
11. The nature of my gratitude? (1-10, record it)
12. My talents and personal strengths? (1-10, record it)
13. The contributions I offer to others? (1-10, record it)
14. My willingness to help? (1-10, record it)
15. The skills I've developed? (1-10, record it)

16. My tech savviness? (1-10, record it)

17. The values I hold and live by? (1-10, record it)

18. My inward fulfillment? (1-10, record it)

19. Having a deeper sense of power? (1-10, record it)

20. The joy I feel? (1-10, record it)

21. Validity of my life received from friends and family? (1-10, record it)

22. My engagement to feel fully and share my emotions? (1-10, record it)

23. Openness to expressing my purpose, grow, create, serve and authentically connect with others. (1-10, record it)

24. My network supports my expression of purpose? (1-10, record it)

25. The congruence of my personal and public life. (1-10, record it)

Tally the final result by adding each value within the Life Purpose sequence, divide by 25 = _____. Record the final result on the circle labeled Life Purpose.

FAITH | SPIRITUALITY

In this section evaluate your Faith | Spirituality by answering: How satisfied am I with..?

1. My awareness of what God means to me? (1-10, record it)

2. God's presence in my life? (1-10, record it)

3. Strength of my faithfulness and respect for God? (1-10, record it)

4. My struggle to have faith and belief in God? (1-10, record it)

5. Understanding what my biggest struggle is with my faith and why? (1-10, record it)

6. Investment I make using my talents? (1-10, record it)

7. My understanding of what's important in life and what isn't? (1-10, record it)

8. The role, beliefs & attitudes about spirituality? (1-10, record it)

9. The comfort I receive? (1-10, record it)

10. My dependency on God? (1-10, record it)

11. My trust in God? (1-10, record it)

12. Expression of my spiritual practice? (1-10, record it)

13. My connections with all things in life? (1-10, record it)

14. Feeling God's love and guidance? (1-10, record it)

15. My love and respect for myself and others? (1-10, record it)

16. Understanding The Lord's Word, the Bible? (1-10, record it)

17. My prayer life? (1-10, record it)

18. My expectations of God—either currently or in the future? (1-10, record it)

19. Understanding what God expects from me? (1-10, record it)

20. My confidence that God will handle all my worries? (1-10, record it)

21. Love, joy, peace, patience, kindness, goodness, faithfulness, gentleness and self-control? (1-10, record it)

22. Thankfulness in ALL things at ALL times? In the blessings and the pain? (1-10, record it)

23. The contributions that faith makes in my life and for my purpose? (1-10, record it)

24. The consistent and meaningful Quiet Time with God, meditation, and prayer? (1-10, record it)

25. The expression, truth, and grace in my relationships? (1-10, record it)

Tally the final result by adding each value within the Faith | Spirituality sequence, divide by 25 = _____. Record the final result on the circle labeled Faith | Spirituality.

TRANSPORTATION | MOBILITY

In this section evaluate your Transportation | Mobility by answering: How satisfied am I with..?

1. The need for a car to be mobile? (1-10, record it)

2. The ease of maintaining and the affordability of my vehicle? (1-10, record it)

3. My ability to drive? (1-10, record it)

4. My driving skills? (1-10, record it)

5. My reaction time when driving? (1-10, record it)

6. My night vision? (1-10, record it)

7. My peripheral vision? (1-10, record it)

8. Sense of safety while driving in heavy traffic? (1-10, record it)

9. Easy access to medical rides or getting to appointments if I can't drive? (1-10, record it)

10. Shopping via foot if unable to drive? (1-10, record it)

11. Acquiring handy rides with friends and neighbors? (1-10, record it)

12. Adequacy of public transit? (1-10, record it)

13. My sense of safety when using public transit? (1-10, record it)

14. Using a taxi service? (1-10, record it)

15. Depending on a ride sharing service? (1-10, record it)

16. Obtaining community medical or health care rides? (1-10, record it)

17. Doable travel long-distance? (1-10, record it)

18. On call transportation services? (1-10, record it)

19. Access healthy food choices? (1-10, record it)

20. Ready special needs mobility? (1-10, record it)

21. Reliable transportation services? (1-10, record it)

22. Making appointments on time? (1-10, record it)

23. Seeking education and volunteer options, employment, and healthcare needs? (1-10, record it)

24. Engaging socially as it relates to transportation? (1-10, record it)

25. Giving social support as it relates to transportation? (1-10, record it)

Tally the final result by adding each value within the Transportation | Mobility sequence, divide by 25 = _____. Record the final result on the circle labeled Transportation | Mobility.

FINANCES | MONEY MATTERS

In this section evaluate your Finances | Money Matters by answering: How satisfied am I with..?

1. Retirement savings? (1-10, record it)
2. Debt and liabilities? (1-10, record it)
3. Capable of paying debt? (1-10, record it)
4. My income? (1-10, record it)
5. Emergency fund? (1-10, record it)
6. Credit score? (1-10, record it)
7. Insurance coverage? (1-10, record it)
8. Social Security? (1-10, record it)
9. Assets? (1-10, record it)
10. Legal docs? (1-10, record it)
11. Checking and savings? (1-10, record it)
12. The amount I need to save each month? (1-10, record it)
13. Potential career opportunities? (1-10, record it)
14. Part-time work? (1-10, record it)

15. Using senior discounts? (1-10, record it)

16. Budgeting? (1-10, record it)

17. Understanding budget management? (1-10, record it)

18. Spending habits? (1-10, record it)

19. Net worth? (1-10, record it)

20. Expenses? (1-10, record it)

21. Tracking income and expenses (1-10, record it)

22. Managing debt? (1-10, record it)

23. Spending less than earned? (1-10, record it)

24. Education? (1-10, record it)

25. Investments? (1-10, record it)

Tally the final result by adding each value within the Finances | Money Matters sequence, divide by 25 = _____. Record the final result on the circle labeled Finances | Money Matters.

LEGAL MATTERS

In this section evaluate your Legal Matters by answering: How satisfied am I with..?

1. My estate planning? (1-10, record it)

2. Power of attorney? (1-10, record it)

3. Financial power of attorney? (1-10, record it)

4. Healthcare directives? (1-10, record it)

5. Wishes will be followed by appointed agents and surrogates? (1-10, record it)

6. Executor? (1-10, record it)

7. Guardianship? (1-10, record it)

8. Will? (1-10, record it)

9. Living Will? (1-10, record it)

10. Long-term care insurance? (1-10, record it)

11. Plan for medical and custodial care costs? (1-10, record it)

12. Emergency contact? (1-10, record it)

13. Documented and have copies of medications and medical problems? (1-10, record it)

14. Copy of insurance cards and ID? (1-10, record it)

15. Copy of house and car deeds? (1-10, record it)

16. Bank statements? (1-10, record it)

17. Passwords? (1-10, record it)

18. Safety deposit box information? (1-10, record it)

19. Organizing and documenting doctors' contact information? (1-10, record it)

20. Organizing and documenting insurance agents' contact information? (1-10, record it)

21. Organizing and documenting business and professional services contact information? (1-10, record it)

22. End of life decisions? (1-10, record it)

23. Burial? (1-10, record it)

24. Body donations? (1-10, record it)

25. Made copies of all above? Selected people know where the originals are stored? (1-10, record it)

Tally the final result by adding each value within the Legal Matters sequences, divide by 25 = _____. Record on the circle labeled Legal Matters.

FUN | ENGAGEMENT

In this section evaluate your Fun | Engagement by answering: How satisfied am I with..?

1. The time I spend smiling? (1-10, record it)
2. The amount of time I laugh with another person? (1-10, record it)
3. Differential of joyful moments minus painful or sad moments? (1-10, record it)
4. Positive experiences? (1-10, record it)
5. Feeling liberated? (1-10, record it)
6. Adaptable? (1-10, record it)
7. Adherence to values? (1-10, record it)
8. Trusting others? (1-10, record it)
9. Comparing myself to others? (1-10, record it)
10. Dancing? (1-10, record it)
11. Sharing a meal? (1-10, record it)
12. Entertaining? (1-10, record it)

13. Invitations out? (1-10, record it)

14. Feeling satisfied and content? (1-10, record it)

15. Willing to try new things? (1-10, record it)

16. Go walking or exercise? Invite others to come along? (1-10, record it)

17. Self-knowledge? (1-10, record it)

18. Exposure to activity calendar? (1-10, record it)

19. Practice gratitude? (1-10, record it)

20. Volunteer? (1-10, record it)

21. Help others out? (1-10, record it

22. G Avoid negative people? (1-10, record it)

23. Plant flowers, learn a new skill, instrument, or hobby? (1-10, record it)

24. Travel? (1-10, record it)

Tally the final result by adding each value within the Fun | Engagement sequence, then divide by 25 = _____. Record on the circle labeled Fun | Engagement.

In the column below tally each result of the particular domain sequence then divide by 25 for the conclusive outcome. Insert your findings.

Final Tally—add values within each domain sequence | record

DOMAIN SEQUENCE	FINAL TALLY (total number of each domain sequence and divide by 25)
HEALTH	FITNESS	
HOUSING	LOCATION	
FAMILY	FRIENDS	CONNECTIONS	
SUPPORT COMMUNITY	
LIFE PURPOSE	
FAITH	SPIRITUALITY	
TRANSPORTATION	MOBILITY	
FINANCES	MONEY MATTERS	
LEGAL MATTERS	
FUN	ENGAGEMENT	

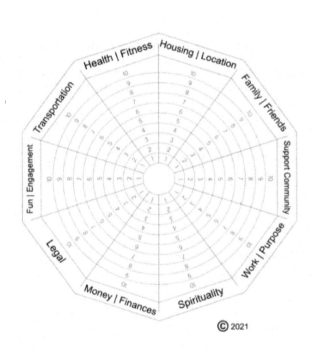

© 2021

CHAPTER 5.
SMART ACTION

You have just completed life's domain assessment! What did you discover? Which domains have the lowest satisfaction scores? Which have the highest? Use the circle on page 46. With a pen, draw on the numbered line matching the final calculation. For example, if the Health and Fitness tallied to 4, draw the line across that number.

Spend time reviewing. Doing so gives indispensable feedback and perhaps will set you in a certain direction. Years ago, when looking at the initial results, I felt off-balance and disorganized. I knew the future, if left unchanged, would be determined by crises. What about you? What's the impression you get looking at the results? What you're shooting for is balance and a well-rounded circle. In balance, you won't blindly analyze and attack each crisis at a time. So, study carefully. It offers hints into potential problems, allowing you a chance to get ahead of trouble.

Act on the factors that influence aging well by exploring the results. When considering each life domain, the scores, and the best course of action—ask yourself: If I had a magic wand and nothing was holding me back, how do I envision the aspect to be in three to five years?

In this chapter, you will take a deep dive into the domains and how the issues of each negatively influence the aspect. If a person can improve the attributes that contribute to the negative effects, then the person has a greater chance in regenerating a better result or outcome. Before the deep dive, let's gain a big picture view of how to think about each life aspect that we want to improve.

SMART HEALTH | FITNESS

Good health is central to well-being. It contributes significantly to prosperity and wealth, as healthy populations are more productive, save more and live longer. For a healthy life cycle, a balanced diet is required: good hygiene habits, staying in a proper shelter and getting enough sleep. During the caregiving years, I noticed that health was the most prized possession. It increases the ability to live at home longer, be more productive, control care and medical expenses, and enjoy friendships and social engagements.

When evaluating your health and fitness, ask: How satisfied am I with my health status and condition? What changes would I like to have? What does the doctor recommend? What choices will I make today to support health? What question, if answered, could make the biggest difference in how I support it? When have I been most satisfied with my health, energy, and vitality? What habits did I practice at that time? How have behaviors altered?

Family Medical History—Know it and Act on it!

Family disease histories are distinct and the risks have varying degrees. While accompanying my parents on medical appointments, I learned about family genetics. When you know the congenial traits early on, you can navigate the threats before disorders take root. Even though we cannot change our genetic makeup, knowing the medical history of our ancestors will mitigate potential diseases.

Launch your assessment by restoring the least satisfying domains. What's your lowest scoring domain? Finances? Health? Housing? Once determined, you're ready to think through each aspect of the life domain circle: review its challenges, recognize and accept the obstacles, research for solutions, and then develop maneuvers that shape a more supportive version. Get your journal, notebook, or a digital document to record your plan of action. Keep in mind: If I had a magic wand and nothing was holding me back, how do I envision life or a specific aspect to be in one, three, and five years?

How well do you know your's? Have you studied it, and how many generations did you include? Always rely on your doctor for feedback. Has your mom or sister had breast cancer? Do/Did your parents, or siblings have diabetes? What about colorectal (colon) cancer before the age of 50? If yes, CDC says you are more likely to get the same disease as your parent or sibling and should consider earlier screening. Talk to your doctor about when to start screening and what other steps to take to prevent or find a threat early.

What are your risks of certain diseases? With a doctor, determine if you need a specific genetic test. Is there a condition you're not aware of? Has your healthcare team procured all preventative medical tests including blood? See the next Chapter Smart Resources for additional information about collecting your family health history.

Collect the Family Health History

Talk to your family—write down the names of your close relatives from both sides of the family: parents, siblings, grandparents, aunts, uncles, nieces, and nephews. Talk to them about the conditions they have or had, and at what age the conditions were diagnosed. The more questions and research you do, the more you'll learn. Questions to ask family members:

- Do you have any chronic diseases, such as heart disease or diabetes, or health conditions, such as high blood pressure or high cholesterol?

- Have you had any other serious diseases, such as cancer or stroke? What type of cancer?

- How old were you when each of these diseases or health conditions was diagnosed? (If your relative doesn't remember the exact age, knowing the approximate age is useful.)

- What is your family's ancestry? From what countries or regions did your ancestors come to America?

- What were the causes and ages of death for the relatives who have died?

A free web-based tool developed by the CDC—My Family Health Portrait is helpful in organizing the information in your family health history. My Family Health Portrait allows you to share this information easily with your doctor and other family members. See the Chapter Smart Resources for the Family Health Portrait.

Update the information when you learn something new. Share what you learn with your doctor and family. If you are concerned about diseases, talk with your doctor at your next visit. Even if you don't know all of the family history, share what you do know, even if incomplete, can help your doctor decide which screening tests are necessary.

Knowing your family's history can direct you in taking appropriate steps that may lower your risk. You can't change your family health history, but you can change unhealthy behaviors. You have the most to gain from lifestyle changes and screening tests.

Annual blood test results and screenings

Regular blood testing is one of the most important ways to keep track of your overall physical health. Getting tested at routine intervals allows the patient to see the way their body changes over time and to make informed decisions.

Blood tests can help the doctor determine how different organs in the body are working: the thyroid, liver, or kidneys. They use blood tests to search for markers of diseases and health conditions like diabetes, HIV, anemia, cancer and coronary heart disease. Even if the patient does not have heart disease, a blood test can show whether they are at risk of developing the condition. See the next Chapter Smart Resources for a good reference to understand blood tests: what they show and more.

Diet and Nutrition

The medical community has long recognized the link between the foods people eat and diseases. Some sources report that it is possible to prevent up to 80 percent of premature heart disease and stroke diagnoses with lifestyle changes: increasing physical activity and healthy eating. You've heard the term, "you are what you eat," but some of the biggest benefits of good nutrition are preventing obesity, a major risk factor for type 2 diabetes, osteoporosis, stroke, heart disease and more, calcium keeps bones strong and prevents osteoporosis, improves mood, which in turn boosts physical activity. Healthy diets raise "good" cholesterol and decrease unhealthy triglycerides.

Diet and nutrition is how I influence my health. Years ago, I ate too much sugar, red meat, and not enough fruit and vegetables. The dietitian recommended a documentary called Forks Over Knives, claiming it changed lives. It altered my perception about food at the opening, "What if everything you believed to be true about most diseases was wrong? Would it change your life? What if it were possible to prevent and reverse symptoms of heart disease, dial down your risk of cancer, stave off type 2 diabetes, sidestep Alzheimer's, and wave away dozens of other conditions that you thought were baked into your DNA?" Forks Over Knives, a documentary.

That was over ten years ago. A plant-based diet remains my go-to meal plan. There are many good ones like the Mediterranean, Paleo,

Vegan, Low-carb and others. The key is to find the one that work for you. Whatever diet you enlist, check with your doctor before making changes. Some health professionals promote a diet rich in olive oil, fruits, vegetables, nuts and fish; low in red meats or processed meats; and includes a moderate amount of cheese and wine. Check with the physician before making any changes to your diet or exercise regime. The first step toward a better diet is finding out where you're already making good choices and where you need improvement. The rules to follow:

1. Eat the correct amount to maintain a healthy weight.
2. Have five servings of fruits and vegetables every day.
3. Include high-fiber foods—whole grains on a daily basis.
4. Consume a variety of foods for adequate vitamins and minerals.
5. Avoid foods that are high in saturated fat or trans-fatty acids (whole milk, fatty meats, snack foods.)
6. Drink eight glasses of water each day.
7. Limit salt and sugar.
8. Limit one (women) or two (men) alcoholic drinks a day.
9. Avoid stress eating.
10. Resist packaged foods, opt for whole, fresh ingredients.

In his book In Defense of Food, Michael Pollan offers three simple, easy-to-remember "rules" for eating:

1. Eat food.

2. Not too much.

3. Mostly plants.

These guidelines are aligned with the 2015 USDA recommendations. See the next Chapter Smart Resources for the links to the USDA Dietary Guidelines and Harvard's Healthy Eating Plate.

Self care routines

Self-care activities are the things that maintain good health and improve well-being. According to Google Trends, the number of searches for "self-care" has more than doubled since 2015.

Use Therapistaid self-appraisal as a guide to evaluate self-care activities and performance. This tool helps a person estimate their self-care needs by spotting patterns and recognizing areas that require attention. See the next Chapter Smart Resources for the links to Therapistaid Worksheets.

Here are self-care pointers that I learned from my doctor and dietitian. Whether they suit you on a daily basis or fulfilling monthly, make it a priority to add a few to feel better.

1. Drink water first thing after waking up

2. Do stretches and yoga poses to get wake the body

3. Do planks and other balance exercises

4. Stop and smell the coffee before guzzling

5. Pray and be grateful

6. Meditate 5 minutes each day

7.   Enjoy a healthy breakfast

8.   Read the Bible

9.   Be easy on yourself—eliminate self-hate talk

10. Change up your walking route at least once a week

11. Check in on friends via text or phone call at least once a week

12. Move your body for 30 minutes if you don't walk

13. Take a hot bath

14. Get plenty of sleep

15. Get negative thoughts on paper (morning pages)

16. Volunteer one hour a month

17. Share a meal with a friend

18. Detox from technology for an hour

19. Workout with a friend

20. Get organized

The Way You Feel about Yourself

When a person doesn't feel good about herself, it's easy to think there's something wrong. Feeling badly is often triggered by the inability to have one's needs met. So, learn what your needs are. Ask yourself:

What people, places, or experiences are must-haves to live fully? What aspects of life—if added—would give a sense of wellness and purpose? What aspects of life—if removed—would deprive a sense of purpose? What steps are needed to feel strong, able, safe, secure, and independent?

If you're having a hard time clarifying your needs, reflect on the times when you weren't content and thriving. What was missing? What bothered you most? Did you?

- Worry about things you can't change.
- Gave up when things got too hard.
- Take yourself too seriously.
- Never exercised.
- Set unattainable goals.
- Eat unhealthy foods often.
- Don't get enough sleep.
- Worry about what others think?
- Stay in your comfort zone.
- Focus on weaknesses not strengths.

Live sincerely, honestly and truthfully—prioritize, focus, communicate your needs, stand up for yourself and let go of everything else, especially the expectations of others.

- Stop being a People-Pleaser
- Be Effective
- Live from the Heart
- Find Purpose
- Forgive Yourself

Forgive yourself—think about the past mistakes, the things you're not so proud of. Each of us has said or done something hurtful, or betrayed someone we care about. Remember that mistakes do not define a person, nor make them good or bad. When a person learns from mistakes—it makes them a better person. See the next Chapter Smart Resources for the links for tips for clarifying needs.

Weight

The National Institute on Health promotes healthy weight because it helps prevent and control disease and conditions. Being overweight or obese has reached epidemic proportions. What's more, as the obesity rate continues to go up, the percentage of Americans actively trying to shed pounds is dropping. Being overweight puts a person at a higher risk of developing serious problems, including heart disease, high blood pressure, type 2 diabetes, gallstones, breathing problems, and certain cancers.

A vast number of adults are satisfied with having larger body sizes, resulting in less motivation to slim down. Feeling attractive and pleasing contributes to self-esteem. But there are additional significant motives to maintain a healthy weight that have nothing to do with looks. See the next Chapter Smart Resources for the links and information on Cost-Effectiveness of Chronic Disease and Healthy Weight Tips for Older Adults.

Fitness

Get up and move more, a new study found that people who weren't as physically active in midlife had smaller brains than their peers 20 years later. Researchers looked at 1,583 men and women who didn't have dementia or heart disease. They worked out on a treadmill to assess their fitness levels. Then, 20 years later, the participants in the study did another treadmill fitness test and had brain scans.

The brain scans revealed that people with a lower exercise capacity, defined as the amount of time on the treadmill before the heart rate hit a certain threshold, were more likely to have smaller brains years later, compared with people who had high fitness levels in middle age. Find the study listed in the Chapter Smart Resources.

Tips for fitness motivation

- Avoiding chronic illnesses is the best motivator for regular physical activity, including endurance, muscle-strengthening, balance, and flexibility exercises.
- Set realistic goals and developing an exercise plan.
- Create and follow the plan. Find an accountability partner to maintain consistency and follow through. Together, come up with an exercise strategy, make it specific, and include type, frequency, intensity, and time. Check progress and re-evaluate goals.
- Get a physical activity tracking tool.

- Check your local community resources, such as mall-walking groups and senior center fitness classes. To find local groups go to Meetup.com, create a neighborhood group on Nextdoor.com, or check with the local senior center and public library for groups nearby. Find more fitness tips in the Chapter Smart Resources.

Emotional health

Biological chemicals have a say in feeling joyful, content, and offering a sense of well-being. The body produces chemicals that mitigate stress and stimulate feelings of content. The inflammatory chemicals produced from excess body fat increase stress-related hormones and interfere with feeling good. Slimming down is just as important for your emotional health as it is for your physical health because obesity increases the risk of depression.

Increase Emotional Well Being

- Find more friends
- Gain self-knowledge — identify your strengths and weaknesses
- Stay active
- Build self-esteem
- Find passion and purpose
- Eat healthy foods
- Drink alcohol moderately
- Set weekly goals

- Learn and set healthy boundaries

Find the emotional wellness tips in the Chapter Smart Resources.

Mobility

Bodies are designed to move. When muscles are working, oxygen and nutrients are pumped throughout the body, keeping the organs healthy and the hormones balanced. Adults who gain weight move less which leads to more weight gain.

Getting older does not mean a person has to give up the physical activities they enjoy. Even if playing competitive soccer or going to the tennis court multiple times a week is no longer safe or feasible, exercise and mobility are still essential. Find modifications or alternatives to physical activities. Shoot for activities that integrate balance, coordination, stretching, strength training, and cardio. Find the Mobility resources in the Chapter Smart Resources.

Chronic Diseases and Managing Them

Chronic disease has the means to cause a fundamental rupture in everyday life, and disrupt the narratives that people hold dear. It can devastate the system and one's ability to take care of themselves. My mother lived with several chronic conditions, and my father lived with the worst one of all, Alzheimer's disease. Helping them navigate the necessary care gave rise to my obsession to plan and to gain solid ground. CDC verifies chronic diseases are defined broadly as conditions that last one year or more and require ongoing medical attention. Chronic diseases such as heart disease, cancer, and diabetes are the leading causes of death and disability in the United States. They are also leading drivers of the nation's $3.8 trillion in annual health care costs.

Lowering the chances of developing chronic issues like high blood pressure, diabetes, is a major motivator to maintain a healthy weight. Too much body fat isn't merely a nuisance, it throws the body's hormones out of whack, bogs down the overall system, and launches unhealthy physiological events that set the stage for chronic conditions. Excess body fat increases inflammation and cell damage, putting older adults at increased risk for cognitive impairment, dementia, rheumatoid arthritis, and osteoarthritis.

Good health ensures independence, security, and productivity. Yet millions struggle every day with health and safety challenges such as chronic disease, falls, and mental health issues—all of which can severely impact quality of life. The National Council on Aging distributes proven programs in-person and online that empower individuals to manage their own care and improve their quality of life. See chronic disease cost study and all resources for managing chronic conditions in the Chapter Smart Resources.

Fracture risk

Older people with broken bones face a higher risk of death, and that risk can stay elevated for years. Hip fractures are known to increase the mortality risk among older people, and this is the first study to identify how long this risk lasts for different fractures. Non-hip fractures contribute to more than two-thirds of all fragility fractures and can include fractures of the femur, pelvis, clavicle or lower leg.

In the year after breaking a hip, men faced a 33 percent higher risk of death and women had a 20 percent higher risk. For femur or pelvic fractures, the one-year excess mortality was between 20 percent and 25 percent. A significant risk of death was still observed 10 years after a person broke a hip, and approximately five years following non-hip fractures.

A FRAX (Fracture Risk Assessment Tool) score indicates the risk of a fracture in a person with osteoporosis. Doctors can use it to determine the best measures to prevent fractures and treat the condition. See Fracture Resources in the Chapter Smart Resources.

Mood

• Benefits of Walking Improves Moods— research shows that regular walks improves the nervous system, leading to decreased levels of anger and hostility. Walking outdoors is even more beneficial: studies have shown that being in nature reduces tension and depression. If you're walking on a treadmill, pull up pictures of natural scenery. Looking at images of nature has been shown to increase emotional stability.

- Lower your risk of lung cancer—Walking reduces your risk of lung cancer by as much as 30 percent. It can also help lessen the severity of symptoms associated with preexisting conditions.
- Skin will look younger—Walking increases the production of collagen and reduces the chances of developing varicose veins. The venous system in the lower half of your legs helps circulate blood and push it back up to the heart and lungs. Walking strengthens leg muscles, which helps improve the venous system's ability to circulate blood.
- Increase Vitamin D levels—Walking outside triggers Vitamin D production. Low vitamin D levels are also linked to depression, frequent illness, fatigue, back pain, slow wound healing, and muscle pain. See Mood Resources in the Chapter Smart Resources.

Sleep

Restorative sleep is crucial for health. If you are overweight, excess fat prevents your lungs from expanding fully, preventing deep breathing which promotes good sleep. Adults age 65 and older need 7-8 hours of sleep to feel rested and alert. But with age, sleep patterns change. Common sleep changes:

- Getting tired earlier in the evening.
- Waking up early in the morning.
- Waking up in the middle of the night and not being able to go back to sleep.

- Having insomnia, which is a condition that makes it hard to fall asleep and/or stay asleep.

If your sleep-wake cycle changes, try these.

- Go to bed and get up at the same time each day.
- Do not take naps longer than 20 minutes.
- Do not read, watch TV, or eat in bed. Only use your bedroom for sleep.
- Avoid caffeine for about 8 hours before bedtime.
- Avoid nicotine and alcohol in the evening. Alcohol might help you fall asleep, but it can cause you to wake up in the middle of the night.
- Do not lie in bed for a long time trying to go to sleep. After 30 minutes of trying to sleep, get up and go to a different room. Do something quiet, read or listen to music. Do not do anything that stimulates your brain. Then, go back to bed and try to fall asleep.
- Try to be active each day. Exercise can help you sleep better.
- Ask your doctor if any of your medicines could be keeping you awake at night. Medicines that can disrupt sleep include antidepressants, beta-blockers, and cardiovascular drugs.

Talk to your doctor if you have trouble sleeping. They will review your symptoms and may run tests to confirm a sleep condition.

Questions to ask the doctor

- How many hours should I sleep each night?
- Could the medicines I take affect my sleep?
- Do I have a health problem that could affect my sleep?
- I seem to sleep fine, but I'm tired all day. What's wrong?
- Is it okay to nap for longer than 20 minutes during the day if I feel I need it?

See Sleep Resources in the Chapter Smart Resources.

Find a Good Doctor

Find a primary care doctor who you feel comfortable with. It's the most important steps to getting good health care. This doctor gets to know you and what your health is normally like. She can help you make medical decisions that suit your values and habits. And recommend other medical specialists and healthcare providers. Make a list of qualities that matter to you. Do you care if your doctor is a man or a woman? Is it important that your doctor has evening office hours, is associated with a specific hospital or medical center, or speaks your language? Do you prefer a doctor who has an individual practice or one who is part of a group so you can see one of the partners if your doctor is not available? After you have made your list, go back over it and decide which qualities are most important and which are nice, but not essential.

Why Geriatricians are Important

Geriatricians are primary care physicians who have specialized training in treating older patients. They can practice in outpatient settings, nursing facilities, or hospitals.

Geriatricians often work as part of a treatment team with other primary care providers, focusing on helping older patients who have multiple health problems or complex conditions. The role of the geriatrician is to coordinate overall care with other physicians and guide the patient in making treatment choices. A geriatrician is helpful if you:

- Suffer from multiple medical conditions
- Find that treatment for one medical condition negatively affects a second condition
- Are experiencing functional decline or physical frailty
- Have a disease associated with aging, such as dementia, incontinence or osteoporosis
- Manage multiple medications (especially if they're causing side effects that interfere with your well-being)

Patients who receive care from a geriatrician in the hospital have better function when discharged. Patients who have specialized geriatrics care in the hospital are also more likely to go directly home after discharge, rather than to rehabilitation centers or nursing homes.

How to Pick a Geriatrician

- Training: Ask whether the geriatrician has received special certifications or training. Also note whether s/he is affiliated with an academic medical center, which generally offers patients the latest advances in care.
- Accessibility: Make sure the practice accepts your insurance. Learn about office hours, who you'll speak to after hours and how the geriatrician manages emergencies. Also inquire whether the geriatrician provides any at-home care services.
- Communication: Find out how the geriatrician coordinates with specialists such as cardiologists, pulmonologists and neurologists. Also ask how he or she prefers to communicate with you: phone calls, electronic portals or face-to-face meetings?
- Philosophy: Make sure you and your geriatrician are on the same page when it comes to your health goals, keeping in mind that those goals may change over time. Also ask what other programs or services he or she might offer. Some geriatricians offer programs for staying healthy, such as exercise classes or fall-prevention education.

Bedside manners are crucial. If you're getting bad vibes, find someone who is a better fit. The same rules apply for therapists, gynecologists, dentists, etc. See Find a Good Doctor Resources in the Chapter Smart Resources.

Health insurance

Do you know the types of health insurance?

Senior Health Care Options and Costs

- Medicare. ...
- Medicaid. ...
- Private Health Insurance Plan. ...
- Supplemental Health Insurance for Seniors Called 'Medigap'
- Health Care Options for Senior Veterans, Military Retirees and Their Spouses. ...
- Assisted Living. ...
- Nursing Homes. ...
- Hospice and End-Of-Life Medical Care.

Improve Functional Ability

Throughout the day, we get out of bed, take baths or showers, use the toilet, dress, prepare meals, and eat. These functions allow us to socialize, work, and engage. They are labeled activities of daily living, or ADLs and reflect our ability to live independently.

Disability or functional impairment refers to one's inability to perform these and other basic tasks without assistance, whether due to aging, illness, accident, or conditions at birth. The most basic ADLs, eating, bathing, dressing, using the toilet, and transferring from bed or chair are distinguished from complex activities—taking medication, managing money, and grocery shopping, which are known as instrumental ADLs—IADLs. They are necessary to live independently in the community: use a telephone, take medications, manage money, grocery shop, prepare meals, perform light and heavy housework, do laundry, use local transportation, and remember appointments.

Consult a physical therapist to create a functional fitness routine tailored to your situation. But if you're (also) looking for ways to train for everyday life on your own, have a look at these ideas.

• Simulate and strengthen your functional skills:

• Stretch—Mobility isn't just about movement, it's about flexibility as well.

• Squats train the same muscles you need to stand up and sit down or pick things up from the floor.

• Lunges in all directions help you do household activities like vacuuming and gardening.

• Step-ups with light weights support your body to climb the stairs with a load of laundry or carry a heavy suitcase. Identify your biggest functional issue and start where you are now, even if that means only doing a 1-minute 'workout' a day.

Ask yourself: Which improvement would make everyday life better?

• To walk to the nearby shops or get back on your bicycle? Then focus on gradually improving your endurance and fitness with brisk walks, low-impact aqua aerobics, dancing in the living room, or interval training for more advanced fitness levels.

- To load groceries in the car, carry a load of laundry up the stairs or pick up your (grand)child? Build total-body strength by practicing squats and lunges, doing push-ups against the wall or simple exercises with resistance bands.

- To get out of the car, bend down to pick things up or reach overhead? Lessen your pain, relax tight muscles, and improve the range of motion with flexibility. Rotate your joints every morning, try touching toes or do yoga, Pilates or tai chi. Just make sure you do a short warm-up first and avoid bouncy stretches.

- To strengthen your legs? Prevent falls by improving balance and coordination. Try walking backwards and sideways, get up from the chair without using your hands, stand on one foot or use a stability ball to train your balance.

Consult your treating physician or a licensed physical therapist for advice before starting a new workout routine. See Improved Functional Ability Resources in the next Chapter for Smart Resources.

SMART HOUSING | LOCATION

Where do you want to call home? In the place you live now or would you prefer to move to a senior housing community? Generally, people choose the place where they've spent the last few decades.

What's your criteria? For me, the top features of a home are: affordable and safe, small-scale, support my health, foster engagement and friendships, and walkable. When researching for the ideal place, I used the AARP's Livable Communities as a reference. Their criteria are access to public transit, walkable and nearby shopping, social engagement, medical and health options, and low crime.

There are numerous considerations when thinking about "home." If you decide to stay where you are, be sure to create a family atmosphere with the neighbors and have connections for companionship. The older you become, social connections are another key component for independence. It contributes a pool of candidates for assistance with decision making, caregiver help, crisis management, a health care surrogate, and a sense of belonging.

Acknowledge and accept your stage in life. Get to know what you will need and plan ahead for the predictable events. Ask yourself: Can I age safely here? Should I remodel? (A care manager can assist you.)What is the age of my home? List all the rooms that need remodeling. Learn how much it will cost. Can I afford it? Could I rent out a room to save money? Can I afford the home maintenance? How important is the location? Do you rent and are you comfortable with being a tenant? What in-home support services are available now, and in the future, to meet my health and social needs? Have I planned for alternative rides? Refer to ADLs in the Improve Functional Ability section of Health | Fitness for the activities of daily living needs to include.

Principles of Aging in Place

Home modifications are physical changes made to a home to adapt for the evolving needs of an older or disabled person that help them remain in place. As people age, the mobility and body strength diminish, making the home more difficult to manage and less functional. Making modifications improves how well the person functions in the home. Even small and simple adaptations from knobs to levers or as comprehensive as the construction of a ramp or granny pad in the backyard.

1. The design is useful to people with diverse abilities.
2. The design accommodates a wide range of individual preferences and abilities.
3. The design minimizes hazards and the adverse consequences of accidental or unintended actions.
4. The design can be used efficiently, comfortably, and with a minimum of fatigue.
5. Appropriate size and space is provided for approach, reach, manipulation, and use regardless of the user's body size, posture, or mobility.

Home Modifications Options—low cost solutions

Removing hazards, such as clutter, throw rugs, moving furnishings and modifying where activities occur (e.g., sleep on first floor instead of second) $0

ADDING FEATURES

Adding non slip strips to floors and smooth surfaces $100-500

Installing home emergency-response units $30-100/month

Improving lighting $50-300/unit

Providing telephones with large numbers and letters $25-100

Installing grab bars and lever door handles $250-1500

MORE COMPLEX FEATURES

Installing ramps $400 - 4,000

Installing chair lifts or stair glides $2,500 - 6,000

Widening doorways $500 - 1,000

Lowering countertops $1,650 - 4,000

Building roll-in showers $700 - 1,000

Remodeling bathrooms $20,000 - 25,000

Improving wiring to eliminate extension cord $8,000 - 15,000

Get a Professional Home Assessment

Hire a Care manager or an Architect to complete an assessment like you would a doctor or a mechanic to ensure you are safe, independent, and are secure in your neighborhood and home. Find a contractor to add modern handrails, door pulls, and hardware elements to stairways, halls and bathrooms. A smart way to consider your home and whether it fits your needs: Make a list of how much time you spend in each room. And then, downsize to a home that has the rooms you use. See the Chapter Smart Resources for links and information about hiring a care manager, architect, and contractor for home modifications.

Housing Options

Questions to Ask About Home Ownership:

- Is remaining at home a short term or a long term plan?
- If I remain at home, how will my social, health and financial needs be met?
- Do I have equity in my home? If so, what are ways to obtain a loan and use it?
- Is house sharing an option?
- Am I eligible for any home repair programs that are completed by volunteers?
- Are there programs available to help me pay for the costs of home repairs, home modifications, home heating expenses, weatherization, utility bills and other expenses of maintaining a home?

Remaining at home may be desirable, choosing that option depends on whether the health, social and financial needs are met.

- Would modifying my home permit me to continue living there? If so, how do I find a qualified remodeler? Is the remodeler I am considering a Certified AginginPlace Specialist? Are there volunteers from my local Area Agency on Aging who can help me?

- What universally designed products and features should I consider to make my home safer and more comfortable?
- Am I eligible for any property tax relief programs in my state?
- Am I eligible for any in home support services through federal, state or local programs, such as Medicare or Medicaid?
- Can I use my long term care insurance policy to pay for in-home support services?

Benefits

✔ Family and friends

✔ House as an asset

✔ Familiar neighborhood ✔ Privacy

Challenges

✔ Maintenance

✔ Possible need for home modifications ✔ Financing

Senior Housing

Some adults want a life filled with planned activities that they share with peers. They pull up stakes to find new companions and amenities in active adult and retirement communities. The communities offer a variety of housing options for purchase or rent. And for homeowners, protecting the home as a financial asset can be very important. They may be counting on it as a future financial resource.

Living in a Group Setting

- Board and Care Homes are private and in residential settings. A board and care home is often a converted or adapted single family home. This type of home provides the following services: a basic room, which may be shared with another person; meals; help with instrumental activities of daily living; the arrangements for or provision of transportation to medical and other appointments; reminders to take medications; and daily contact with staff. Services such as meals, supervision and transportation are usually handled by the home's owner or manager.

- Adult Foster Care Homes provide room, board and in-home support services in a family setting. Generally, an adult foster care home provides more in-home support services than a board and care home. These homes may meet the needs of adults who require periodic or regular assistance with activities of daily living. Some adult foster care homes may offer more complex care if the staff has experience and is trained to provide it. In some cases, visiting nurses provide the necessary assistance.

- Adult Care Facilities provide room, board and in home support services to six or more adults who are not related to the operator. Services for residents may be similar to a board and care home or an adult foster care home. Adult care facilities generally have more residents. They are therefore less likely to resemble family life. Adult care facilities may also be called congregate housing. They're available for older adults who are no longer able or willing to live completely independently. Generally, residents live in a private apartment and are capable of getting to the communal dining area independently. They usually receive help with grocery shopping, meal preparation and housework.

- Residential Care Facility is a group residence that provides each resident with, at a minimum, assistance with bathing, dressing, and help with medications on a 24 hour day basis. The facility may also provide medical services under certain circumstances.

- A Life Plan Community formerly known as a Continuing Care Retirement Community, is a residential community for active, independent adults aged 60+ that provides a variety of living options, along with services, amenities and a continuum of care designed to address the changing needs of residents as they age.

- Assisted living Community give residents personalized care in a residential setting. They're for seniors whose health or well-being requires a higher level of support, which is determined through a health assessment by the community according to state regulations. Assisted living also provides a healthy lifestyle and social engagement. The most common assisted living services offered include medication management and assistance with using the bathroom, dressing and grooming. Housekeeping, meals, laundry and transportation services, as well as social programs and activities, are typically included. Staff is available 24/7 to help with safety, care and support. Residents are encouraged to bring furniture and personal items to make their new home feel, well, like home.

- Skilled Nursing Facility is an in-patient rehabilitation and medical treatment center staffed with trained medical professionals. They provide the medically-necessary services of licensed nurses, physical and occupational therapists, speech pathologists, and audiologists.

Benefits: Group housing options offer a wide range of in-home support services, a variety of housing types and the choice of location of facilities. They also give residents opportunities for socializing with others.

Questions to Ask About Group Housing:

- What is the basic monthly rate and what in-home support services are included in that rate? How many hours of service are included?
- Can I save hours that I do not use during a day or week for a later time when I do need them?

- Is there an entrance fee? Is it refundable?
- Is there a waiting list?
- Am I eligible for any in home support services through federal, state or local programs?
- Can I use my long term care insurance policy to pay for in-home support services?
- Can I purchase additional services? If so, what types of services and how many hours a day or week are they available? What would those additional costs be and how would I be billed?
- What happens if my needs change or increase?
- Will I be asked to sign an admissions agreement or a contract before I move in? Are there resources available to help me understand the contract?
- Are my utilities included?
- How will I be assigned a room? Can I bring my own furnishings?
- Can I have a pet?
- Will the facility honor my special food and dietary preferences?
- Can I have guests in my unit?
- What is the provider's background and experience? Is the provider financially sound?
- What are the professional qualifications for staff and how many people does each staff person serve?

- What are the training requirements for the facility administrator and for the staff?
- Is the facility close to shopping, senior centers, religious facilities, medical facilities and other amenities that are important to me?
- Do rooms have a telephone and television? How is billing for those handled?
- Does the facility have safety features? Does it have a disaster relief plan?
- What happens if the facility asks me to leave?
- Have I received a copy of the facility's statement of resident rights?
- Is there a resident council? Can I participate in facility management and decision making?

Additional housing ideas

- 55+ Housing

A 55+ or Active Adult community is a community designed specifically for individuals age 55 and older. Everything from floor plans and expected home maintenance to community events and resources cater to older homeowners. These communities are also age-restricted, meaning residents have to meet the 55+ requirement in order to purchase a property. However, there are some exceptions to this rule.

- Cohousing

Cohousing is a small intentional community of private homes clustered around a shared space, which usually includes a large kitchen, dining area and recreational areas. Neighbors get together to maintain their shared space, plan community activities, eat meals and lend a helping hand to one another when needed. In nearly every Cohousing community, the management is handled democratically by residents who live on the property.

Choose Your Lifestyle

Lifestyle trends for adults, retirees and younger, will be different since they expects to live longer than any previous generation. The question, "Will those years be vigorous and healthy, or will they be spent living in pain and disability of chronic disease?" A lot hangs on the answer because the widespread obesity among adults, combined with lack of exercise, could lead to an epidemic of diabetes, which dramatically accelerates aging and leads to a host of diseases. If a person joins the fragile, dependent population, they will place tremendous demands on Medicare, and require lots of support from professional caregivers and family.

Other signs suggest that older adults will enjoy better health as well. Furthermore, they may age more slowly because of healthy habits. Gary Burtless, a senior fellow at the Brookings Institution, believes, "The influence of aging on society depends on which view you accept, longer life spans would be a burden if additional years were spent in a frail, dependent condition, but I don't hold that pessimistic view. I think there's a lot of evidence that people are healthier mentally and physically than they used to be."

Remaining vigorous and healthy, requires intention, conviction, and knowing what you want. Ask yourself: What kind of lifestyle do I want? What are my preferred living conditions?

Think about what you DON'T want—If you ask, "what will make me happy," you'll be confused. Instead, think about what makes you unhappy, and then about how you can create a life that avoids as many of those dissatisfactions as possible. It's another way to find your sweet spot—anticipate what's not working to uncover what would work better.

Focus on Experiences—think about the kinds of experiences you want to have and what a life with those experiences would look like. For example, I know I like traveling, whether it's to visit friends, see new places, or just have a change of scenery. So my lifestyle needs to support that. Another example, I adore walking. How can the location where I live support my traveling on foot?

Experiment More—You need a large data set to know what you like and don't like. Play around more, try new things, be willing to fail, and as you gain more exposure to different options you'll get a better sense of what you like and don't like. For example, on the recommendation of a friend I went to an online Pilates class. Turns out it was fun.

Plan an Ideal Week—Consider an ideal day or week living where you are now or where you want to live. If you're not sure what to fill in, then think back on some of your best days that were productive, satisfying, creative, and fulfilling? What happened? What makes them stand out?

Think About The Activities You Want to Do—There needs to be some fun in your life, but you also have to plan for the things that aren't so pleasant. First, start with the types of activities that get you jazzed up? When you think about it, Netflix is most likely not something that you consider super fun, but something you do to veg out for a while. What do you find seriously fun that you want more of in your life? Include activities that might seem hard to do like sailing, hiking, or traveling to another country. If that's what you find fun and want more of in your life, then find a way to make it happen. Next consider the things you need, like rides when you can't drive, someone to check on you when ill, and connections to avoid isolation and loneliness.

Taking Action—This isn't something you write down once and then go on with your life. At the back of your mind, consider: "What kind of life do I want," and "Is what I'm doing right now in line with that idea of an ideal life?" Ask yourself, "What is one thing I can do today to improve my well-being, to meet a new person, to volunteer my time, or learn a new skill?"

Location of the Home

Neighborhood matters when it comes to how satisfied we are with a house or apartment. Depending on how well social and physical aspects of the environment fit our personal resources and attitudes, places can influence our well-being. Because living in places we like, where we function well, and which offer opportunities for social, physical, and mental stimulation can benefit our health and quality of life no matter our age. Identifying factors:

Transportation—If you prefer not to drive or can't drive but need to get somewhere, make sure the neighborhood or suburb has robust public transit that runs when you need it. And use Walk Score to gauge the neighborhood's walkability or ease of getting around when stuck without a car.

Town or City Size—If you prefer the comforting cloak of anonymity to the glare of the small-town spotlight? You're a natural fit for big-city life. Or if you enjoy seeing folks you know around town every day and patronizing businesses whose proprietors know exactly what you want —you're a small-town person at heart. But the question is, what do you want? In general, small town life is slower, often more affordable, but with less opportunities and less convenience. Meanwhile, living in a large city is fun, exciting, but definitely more expensive and challenging —such as congested traffic and driving in it. Things to consider:

Crime rate, safety and security—smaller towns are always the safest but it depends on the local government and how much they spend on law enforcement. Besides, immediate care services are another concern. Every city has its "safe zones." Long-time residents in metropolitan areas know where to avoid at night and what neighborhoods they should steer away from.

Cost Of Living—but consider the growth opportunities as well. Everyone wants to save on living expenses, but seek out balance instead. If extremely low spending leads to a life whose sole purpose is to save but not to enjoy, then you may not prefer that route.

Work—whether part-time or full-time, the labor market, generally in smaller towns, is less competitive. And they're better for smaller businesses and other less competitive markets. Bigger ones have robust, high-end and advanced jobs, especially in the technology, public relations or more business-centric markets. Local labor markets typically are less competitive in smaller towns. Nowadays, the job markets caused by the differences between small and big cities are less extreme, due to the uprising of work-from-home and other remote possibilities. Another factor, online work is a huge attraction for folks working from home so, it doesn't matter where one lives! Online possibilities: Bookkeeper, Freelance writer, Social media manager, Online tutor, Recruiter, Digital marketer, Proofreader, Website designer, Facebook Ads Specialist, SEO Expert, Graphic designer, Data entry, Virtual assistant, and more!

Affordable shopping—small towns aren't always less costly. According to a survey conducted by NDSU, an exact bag of groceries costs 21% less in national chain stores (Walmart, ALDI, etc) compared to local, neighborhood-owned stores that are more frequently-seen in small towns.

Affordable homes and rent—Real estate in big cities increase more than in small towns because urbanization drives demand. The question to ask: Whether the price increase can justify a higher mortgage, real estate tax etc. Of course, owning expensive real estate in big cities, you might also have a bigger risk in case of a housing market crash. Rents are a big consideration when deciding between small vs. big areas. I've lived in both and by far, the bigger cities' housing and rental properties are higher than the smaller towns.

The federal Department of Housing and Urban Development (HUD) defines an "affordable dwelling" as one that a household can obtain for 30 percent or less of its income. But this varies from city to city. How much of your monthly budget does your home consume each month? Can you handle the home maintenance and it's upkeep? Do you rent and are you comfortable with that? "Affordability" encompasses the total cost of living — not just housing costs, but expenditures like utilities, property taxes, real estate value, groceries, durable goods, and health care.

Options for Affordable Housing:
- Section 8 housing
- Some non profit senior living communities
- Rent a room

- Rent a granny pad
- Share or buy a home with a trusted friend of family member

Entertainment, Recreation and Culture—big cities offer a variety of dining, live music, nightlife, state fairs, seasonal events, world-class museums and theaters, and professional sports teams. Ask yourself: "Do I prefer traveling to events or do I want all the fun right at my doorstep?" Small towns are family-oriented. When it comes to activities, think church gatherings, small-scale town fairs, and local amenities. But if you enjoy outdoor activities that require ample space or proximity to nature, such as hunting and camping, or want plenty of property to raise crops and livestock, stick to the wide-open spaces.

Infrastructure—Healthcare—Less developed areas whether it's small towns or rural, both have insufficient access to healthcare. Whatever the event, if the closest emergency care is 20-30 minutes away, that is significant. When it comes to the inconveniences created by small towns, things become serious. For one, it is nearly mandatory that you have a car and are comfortable for long periods of driving on a regular basis.

Health services—Generally speaking, major metropolitan areas have more health care choices and coverage than thinly populated parts of the country, though localized disparities are quite common within metro areas. Smaller towns and cities with major research universities or hospitals typically punch above their weight as well, so keep those in mind when doing research. Large cities have multiple emergency care rooms and centers and an ambulance will pick you up if needed. In less urgent issues, you can probably go around the block to a pharmacy and handle things yourself. However, metropolitan areas have public transportation. A lot of places are within walking distance as well. Even if you don't have a car, you can get by living in an urban area where shopping and healthcare are within walking distance.

*Don't ignore mid-city living—especially the ones with larger universities. Most offer lower priced living while offering more amenities than the smaller communities.

Climate—Whether you're dreaming of tropical temperatures in South Florida, hoping for the dry heat in Phoenix or aiming for ocean breeze in Southern California, you have to determine which climate will be the best fit. It's worth noting that climate impacts more than just our physical comfort, mental health, hobbies, and what we wear. It very often shapes local economies and, by extension, employment and relocation decisions.

- Considering climate and affordability, Southeast cities are the leading options.
- North Carolina hubs Charlotte and Raleigh are the best choices for home buyers looking for affordable housing and year-round mild weather.

- People looking for warmer climates and gentle winters can find affordable options in the Sunbelt.
- Philadelphia is the top choice for home buyers who want to avoid scorching summer temperatures. (Source: PropertyShark.com)

Airport—Frequent travelers find convenience when living close to an airport. Neighborhoods close to airports have convenient public transportation, which make trips easier. Other benefits are access to all parts of the city, high economic activity, good quality of life, and multiple residential options. Ask yourself: How important is it for me to live within 30 miles of an airport? What was the total number of times you traveled via air in the last 1, 3 and 5 years? Answer the same traveling via a vehicle?

Proximity to Family and Friends

When was the last time you made a new friend? Not just a new acquaintance but someone really close—a person to call in an emergency? If you're older, you may have noticed it's harder to make lifelong relationships. But to be surrounded by friends and peers who are central to your network increases the chances of a satisfying and supportive future. The Framingham Heart study discovered: Having a friend who lives within a mile increases happiness by 25%. Similar effects are seen in co resident spouses, 8%, siblings who live within a mile 14%, and next door neighbors 34%. Effects are not seen between coworkers. The effect decays with time and with geographical separation. See the study in Smart Resources, Proximity to Friends.

Benefits of Nearby Friends

- Friends meet our need for support beyond what families provide.
- True friendship offers a unique feeling of connection that cushions stress.
- Social ties reduce risk of disease by lowering blood pressure, heart rate and cholesterol.
- Serves as a barrier to Alzheimer's disease, obesity and lower immunity.

The Nurses' Health Study from Harvard Medical School found that the more friends women had, the less likely they were to develop physical problems. The results were so significant, the researchers concluded that not having close friends is as detrimental to health as smoking or obesity. See the study in Smart Resources, Benefits of Nearby Friends.

The In-Home Support Services—Age in Place Self-Assessment

Aging in place is the process of staying at home as you grow older instead of moving to an outside facility. To age in place safely and independently, create a budget, discuss options with family and friends, connect with home health services and identify necessary home modification projects. Aging in place works best when there's a plan to modify the home and establish a supportive network of family and friends, and care services.

Ask yourself? Can I age safely here? Should I remodel to stay safe? (A care manager can assist you.) What is the age of the home? List all the rooms that need to be remodeled. How much will that cost? Can you afford it? Who will help you keep up the maintenance and bills? Can you rent out a room to help save money? Can you afford your home maintenance? How important is your choice of location? Do you rent and are you comfortable with that? What in-home support services are available now, and in the future, to meet your health and social needs? Does my community offer innovative community-based housing services such as a Village to Village Network and Naturally Occurring Retirement?

Evaluate your in-home needs

Use this checklist—it lists the things you may need; meals, medical assistance and/or housing.

- Dress and undress without help?
- Drive or use public transportation on your own?
- Shop for groceries or clothing on your own?
- Prepare meals?
- Take a bath or shower without help?
- Be left alone during the day?
- Pay bills and manage finances on your own?

- Take care of yourself?
- Maintain a healthy weight?
- Manage medications?
- Clean the house or apartment?
- Manage household duties?
- Live alone comfortably and confidently?
- Remain active and interested in life and hobbies?
- Keep a strong positive attitude?
- Walk, climb stairs and can get around the house easily?
- Care about your own personal health and well-being?

Go to the Chapter Smart Resources for In-Home Support Services—Age in Place Self-Assessment.

Other tips:

- Talk with your doctor about your concerns about being safe at home.
- Consider meeting with a geriatric care manager to have a formal assessment performed.
- A geriatric care manager or care coordinator can perform a professional assessment of your current quality of life.
- Look into home modifications and products that could help you get around more easily.

Things to do to remain safely at home: Hire a Care manager or an Architect for an assessment like you would a doctor or a mechanic to ensure you are safe, independent, and at peace with your neighborhood and home. Find a contractor to add modern handrails, door pulls, and hardware elements to stairways, halls and bathrooms. Make a list of how much time you spend in each room. Downsize to a home that has the rooms you use. Check the local resources for a Village to Village Network for neighborly services.

Household Monthly Budget

Plan and track spending through budgeting as long as you accurately account for all the bills you need to pay. So before you start plugging numbers into a spreadsheet or app, take a minute to list out each of your monthly expenses.

Needs

- Mortgage/rent.
- Homeowners or renters insurance.
- Property tax (if not included in the mortgage payment).
- Auto insurance.
- Health insurance.
- Out-of-pocket medical costs.
- Life insurance.
- Electricity and natural gas.
- Water.
- Sanitation/garbage.

- Groceries, toiletries and other essentials.
- Car payment.
- Gasoline.
- Public transportation.
- Internet.
- Cell phone and/or landline.
- Other minimum loan payments.

Savings and Debt

- Emergency fund.
- Savings account.
- 401(k).
- Individual retirement account.
- Other investments.
- Credit card payments (see budget tip below).
- Extra payments on mortgage.

Wants

These are harder to account for in a budget because they don't come with a set monthly fee. Wants should account for up to 30% of your spending.

- Clothing, jewelry, etc.
- Dining out.
- Special meals in (steaks for the grill, etc.).
- Movie, concert and event tickets.

- Gym or club memberships.
- Travel expenses (airline tickets, hotels, rental cars, etc.).
- Cable or streaming packages.
- Self-care and personal grooming, like spa visits.
- Home decor.

See more Location Resources in the next Chapter Smart Resources.

SMART CONNECTIONS | FRIENDS

Social connection and engagement are closely related to home and location. Family has been the common social network but it's shrinking; fewer children and grandchildren are available to provide oversight. It's not the same as it was twenty years ago when older folks like my parents relied on offspring. Today, even social circles dwindle. A member of the Elder Orphan Facebook Group spent 30 years working in the hospitality industry. He, like many, never made friends outside the job. Now he's retired and very lonely.

The U.S. Census 2018 estimates more than 15 million adults, or nearly one in six Americans aged 55 and older, are childless, and the levels of childlessness among adults are expected to increase. If there's insufficient social exchange, relationships are thwarted and sets off social inactivity.

AARP's research on Livable Communities was my initial go-to resource. I knew the odds of aging well in the suburbs would be tenuous. I researched the consequences of increased social isolation, greater dependence on automobiles for mobility and independence, and the financial vulnerability associated with housing expenses.

Cathy Cress, Geriatric Care Manager, CathyCress.com, suggests, "Learning how to increase "quality of life" intellectually, spiritually, emotionally and physically as you age is most significant. Seek ways to have joy and mental happiness at every stage. For the single person without family, it is critical." Cress recommends taking preventive steps by doing an assessment of what brings you happiness and joy. Write down what you like to do—quilting, creative-intellectual, basketball, physical, visit with your "family of choice" or kin, emotional, go to church or a synagogue, or pray, spiritual.

> More to the point, put yourself in an environment where there are peers you're drawn to. Whether it's a faith organization, a Bible study, mastermind group, a sports league, walking group, yoga class, a class at a community college, a cooking class, a MeetUp or a Facebook group… go where you'll meet multiple new people.

In the Elder Orphan Facebook Group, we talk about the significance of social connections. Remarkably, I've read about one member driving to the ER after an accident at home. She was scared and worried. It's good that she made it safely but it's not prudent when in an emergency. Each of us will face emergency situations at some point, it's imperative we have friends to count on for help. If you have few friends, make a plan to find more.

Assessing Friendship

Ask yourself? Do I gravitate to people who enjoy the same activities as I do? Do I spend most time with peers who share similar beliefs? Or, do I mix things up? Am I willing to try a variety of new things? Am I comfortable around people who challenge my beliefs, traditions, and make me question my own beliefs and traditions? Do you enjoy being with people who don't share similar political or religious beliefs? How willing am I to have impromptu conversations with strangers? Do I cut myself off from them in fear that they're trying to sell me something? Does the feeling of awkwardness stand in my way of connecting with people I don't know?

While exploring ways to meet new friends, be open to connecting with all ages!

Daily Social Interactions

Strong relationships impact our physical health and mental well-being. The American Public Health Association says healthy relationships lead to better lives. Whether you're retired or still working, it's important to be intentional when creating relationships.

- Brainstorm places to meet people: classes at the gym, MeetUp groups, church or other religious venues, volunteer groups, neighborhood events, and community events.

- Think about your favorite hobbies and join a group that supports the interest (hiking and walking club, Friends of the Library, the local gardening club.)
- My preferences are political MeetUp groups, a trivia night at my community's club room, a dance event at the local adult center, a game night at my house, and cooking a meal at the outdoor BBQ terrace, walking with neighbors, and attending online lifelong classes.
- Have a strong intention to meet new people when socializing. Make it a point to go on coffee dates during the week, meet for Sunday brunch, or attend a monthly club meeting.
- Consider men and women of all ages as potential friends. Nurture friendships with people of all ages—you will stay energetic and engaged.
- Take the initiative. Be open to friendly conversation and take the first step towards friendship.

Where to Find Friends—Activities are the hot spot. Attend political, religious/faith, sports, fitness, in-person or online classes, game groups, social or other groups. If you enjoy reading, check out book clubs. Or board game groups, if that's an interest. Think about the past, where have you met friends before? Do you have a favorite hobby like gardening, chess, knitting, sewing, painting, tennis, golf, writing, cooking or reading? Do you have special skills to share—could you teach a class?

Make New Friends

Answer: What is a friend to you, list the qualities and characteristics of them? (Suggested list: sense of humor, willing to share and be shared with, interesting and interested, good listener, engaged in fitness or learning new things, enjoys window shopping, browsing open houses or estate sales, sharing worldwide religious and political goings on, eating out or cooking in, travels, living or working within a 30-minute radius.) What do you value most in a friend? What does friendship mean to you? Are you comfortable starting conversations in natural settings—the supermarket, the place you worship, the library, college extension classes, the local senior centers, at the gym, or in the park?

Friendships have an impact on our mental health and happiness—even longevity. One Swedish study found that, along with physical activity, maintaining a rich network of friends can add significant years to your life. But close friendships don't just happen. Many of us struggle to meet people and develop quality connections. Whatever the age or circumstances, it's never too late to meet new companions, reconnect with old ones, and to improve your social life, emotional health, and overall well being.

Deepen the sense of belonging

Increase the sense of belonging by seeking out the similarities, instead of focusing on ways you're different.

- Identify who is most important to you—make a list of close friends. Who are the essential people who have your back? You can have all types of relationships in life, but you need to know which each relationship gives you—loyalty, trust, compassion, or laughter and fun. You'll create a sense of belonging if your relationships give you what you need. Prioritize the relationships that meet it.

- Make a difference by contributing to the lives of others.

- Does anyone in your life have a different belief system? Enjoy a good debate or share a similar value—faith in God. Share your differences and still accept that the person creates peace. Acceptance does not mean agreement. To accept others and views that are not the same as yours may require that you value another's way of thinking.

- Cultivate relationships by being fully present, asking questions, giving time, and listening to what the other person has to say. Relationships require two people to make them meaningful. Make sure you're not the one that's holding them back.

- Avoid the false notion of individualism—and "making it on your own." In reality, belonging is the most essential component of a meaningful life.

- Communicate acceptance through validation. Validation builds a sense of belonging and strengthens relationships. By acknowledging someone's internal experience helps you stay or the same side, offering a sense of belonging, even when you disagree.

- Say yes to opportunities to be with others and then throw yourself into whatever the activity is. Being curious allows you to look at your life through an optimistic lens. Obstacles and challenges become a means of learning, rather than a setback or failure. Ask yourself, "What did I learn from this? How can I grow from here?"
- Let go of judgments, they build walls. Focus on people. Connecting with others is far more important. It's far better to make personal connections than to worry about what others think of you. Stop isolating until you believe you are worthy. No one is perfect. We all have struggles.
- Develop self-awareness to feel a sense of belonging. Get to know yourself better and learn what drives you.

Connections for the Heart

We experience emotion as a direct and immediate result of our involvement and interaction with the world. Emotional connection can mean different things but here are the basics that apply.

- Subjective feelings create a bond between two individuals.
- Arousing strong feelings: anger, sorrow, joy, love or any other emotions that humans experience.
- Bond, a link or tie to something or someone.

Developing emotional connections enable bonds, the kind that provokes safety and acceptance. Having connections like these will boost a sense of worth, value, and respect. Review and think how you can create more of the following with one or several friends.

Ask yourself: Can I get the attention of a friend when I need it? When I ask for a friend's attention, are they available to me? Does s/he listen and hear what I'm saying? Am I a top priority to her/him when together? Are my close connections accessible? Can s/he comfort me when I am anxious, sad, lonely, or afraid? Will s/he make some effort to comfort me in those situations? Is s/he responsive to me? Do they care about my well-being even when we are not together? Will they care about me consistently and reliably? Are we truly engaged in each other's lives?

Shared values of true friends

- Shared trust
- Understanding
- Share dreams
- Acceptance
- Be supportive
- Be genuine
- Make the relationship a priority
- Listen and express feelings

Find Daily Social Interactions Resources in the Chapter Smart Resources.

Shared Support in the Hard Times

As the saying goes, "Surround yourself with the people you want to be like." Successful people want to surround themselves with successful people. Optimists like to be around optimists. How can you tell if you're hanging around with the right group of friends who will be there for you? Here are 10 questions to ask yourself to know if you're surrounded by good friends who care.

1. Do they listen? A good friend knows when you need an ear, someone to listen for a few minutes to talk something through. More importantly, they collaborate with you—offering solid, actionable ideas and where they think you're off base.

2. Do they care? Good friends take the time to ask about your life, interests, and your opinions. They're there for you when you need them and want to help.

3. Do they have your best interests at heart? You may not always agree but good friends look out for each other. Even when you don't agree, good friends will support whatever you decide to do, within reason. They may not agree or like what you're doing, like moving across the country to be close to family, but they'll be there to help you pack.

4.   Do your friends lie? When the chips are down and you really need to be told the truth, good friends may hate it…but they tell the truth.

5.   Do they check in on you? If they don't hear from you periodically, they pick up the phone or send a text, "Hey, where are you? Everything okay?"

6.   Do your friends come with a balance sheet? You shouldn't always have to reciprocate. A good friendship doesn't come with a balance sheet. However, people should try to give as good as you get from others. It doesn't mean you or they should feel obligated every single time.

7.   Can you call your friends anytime you need them? This does not mean three in the morning, unless it's an emergency. However, during the hours when you know they're awake, you can call, "Hey…you got a few minutes? I need an ear."

8.   Are you there for your friends? Do they feel like they can call you when they need you? Part of being a good friend is being available, and this applies just as much to you as it does your friends.

9.   Do your friends tell you when you're making a mistake? It can be difficult to hear that you've made a mistake. A true friend is able to say you're making a mistake without anyone feeling hurt or shamed.

10. Do they judge you? A friend doesn't make you question your own character, intelligence, beliefs, decisions or preferences in a way that causes shame.

By putting in the time and effort to maintain your relationships, you will enjoy the positive returns from the strong connections you have with the people in your life.

1. Make friends where you are. Introduce yourself to neighbors, start a conversation with them when outdoors. Invite a neighbor for a walk or a cup of coffee. Relationships are easier to establish and maintain if they start where you already are.

2. Break out of your comfort zone. Arrange to do something with a new friend that falls outside of the same-old and do something that interests you both. It doesn't matter if you go shopping, out to lunch, or take a cooking class. The idea is to share a new experience, which studies show can enhance bonding.

3. Make time for hobbies. Whether you enjoy yoga or reading, get out of the house to do the activities you're crazy about. While many of these hobbies are individual pursuits, there's no reason you can't enjoy them with other people. Find a meet-up group for cooking, or trying out new restaurants. There are meetups that allow solitary knitters to ply their needles in groups rather than solo. The key is forging friendships around an activity you're already doing.

4.   Ask for help. If you never ask friends for favors, you rob them of a two-way, give-and-take relationship. The "I-can-do-it-all" mentality hurts you (because no one can actually do it all!), and it hurts current and future friends, because everyone wants to feel needed and valued. Need someone to run a quick errand for you? That's a great way to test the waters.

5.   Reach out on social media. If you've fallen out of touch with friends from high school, college or a former job, consider reaching out to them on social media. It's a fun way to re-establish old friendships.

SMART SUPPORT COMMUNITY

Close and caring relationships are undeniably linked to health and well-being at all stages. Relationships provide a foundation for coping with adversities and a platform to connect with friends, neighbors, and peers who live nearby and are willing to be there for one another. But the time to build a team of support is before you need a hand. It's not fair to expect a new friend to take care of you or give you a ride to the doctor if they have known you for a short time.

My single friends frequently discuss tough issues and share resources, words of encouragement, and tips that help each other to get by. I believe if one has a family member closeby, it's easier for them to face a challenge, an impending medical treatment, and even a hospital stay. But what do you do if you don't have someone dependable to rely on?

Ask yourself: Do I have friends who live nearby? Would I consider one or two of my neighbors as friends? Am I comfortable asking for favors or help? If I were sick, who would I call for help with an urgent need? Is there someone I can turn to for advice about a problem? If I had to go out of town for a few weeks, who could I call to look after my house or apartment (the plants, pets, garden, etc?) If I were stranded 10 miles from home, is there a person to call who could come and get me? What would I do if I got sick and couldn't cook or run to the store for food? What about getting to a doctor's office? If I can't drive, how would I get there?

Build a Support Team

If you're a single person with no family nearby, you may be satisfied with the status quo and content with being alone. Perhaps you do everything for yourself and like it that way. That's partly good and partly shaky because in older age, you'll need people around, those you trust and can rely on.

Building support for help and to offer help in return requires a network of people, the trusted kind. People need to feel a sense of belonging to a larger social group and to feel connected with them. By putting in the time and effort to maintain relationships, you will enjoy the positive returns from the strong connections.

1. Make friends where you are. Introduce yourself to neighbors, start a conversation when outdoors. Invite a neighbor for a walk or a cup of coffee. Relationships are easier to establish and maintain if they start where you already are.

2. Break out of your comfort zone. Arrange to do something with a new friend that falls outside of the same-old and do something that interests you both. It doesn't matter if you go shopping, out to lunch, or take a cooking class. The idea is to share a new experience, which studies show can enhance bonding.

3. Make time for hobbies. Whether you enjoy yoga or reading, get out of the house to do the activities you're crazy about. While many of these hobbies are individual pursuits, there's no reason you can't enjoy them with other people. Find a meet-up group for cooking, or trying out new restaurants. There are meetups that allow solitary knitters to ply their needles in groups rather than solo. The key is forging friendships around an activity you're already doing.

4. Ask for help. If you never ask friends for favors, you rob them of a two-way, give-and-take relationship. The "I-can-do-it-all" mentality hurts you (because no one can actually do it all!), and it hurts current and future friends, because everyone wants to feel needed and valued. Need someone to run a quick errand for you? That's a great way to test the waters.

5.   Reach out on social media. If you've fallen out of touch with friends from high school, college or a former job, consider reaching out to them on social media. It's a fun way to re-establish old friendships.

Tips for giving support

- Find a time to talk - even a few minutes will sustain connection.
- Listen to them – just listening can make a huge difference to how someone feels.
- Comfort them – there isn't a wrong thing to say.
- Encourage them to find support - remind the friend that seeking help is a sign of strength.
- Do the things you both enjoy together – sometimes just doing the normal things you do together like watching a video or going for a walk can make a big difference to how they're feeling.
- Keep in contact – ask them how they're doing, keep inviting them to join in, and keep sending the occasional message just to check in, even if they don't reply.
- Do something nice – like just sending a message to make them smile or laugh, or plan something small, something to look forward to, like a lunch out.
- Be patient – your friendship might feel different for a while, but there will still be good times and they will be glad if you can stick by them.

Assistance from Experts and Professionals

- Aging Life Care Professionals (also known as geriatric care managers) specialize in aging and disabilities. Through consultation, assessment, care coordination and advocacy, an Aging Life Care Professional works with clients and families to address these challenges.

- Patient Advocates assist adults with locating a new doctor or specialist, checking on patients recovering in the hospital, confused about medications and concerned about allergic reactions, navigating the clinical trial landscape, or securing financial resources for treatments.

- Dietitians for nutrition and information.

- A physical and occupational therapist helps with physical pain and improves movement.

- A nurse is a good resource for good health practices.

- A primary care physician will help you put the pieces together. See a specialist for specific diseases like heart, diabetes, arthritis, dementia, or cancer.

- Local fire departments schedule home safety checks, including smoke alarm installation.

- Pharmacists are the most accessible health care practitioner. They give drug information. Drug/supplement/food interactions, monitor use and act as a liaison between physicians and patients.

- In-home caregivers provide personal care services that range from a few hours a day to around-the-clock live-in care.

Find Expert and Professional Resources in the Chapter Smart Resources.

Support groups

It takes a village to help an older person. Even with three loving daughters, the number of hands fell to meet all the demands my parents needed. If an older person doesn't have family to count on, they will need a village, a community of people who care. One can accomplish a safe and even thriving lifestyle aging alone if they have a collection of individuals who merge for common purpose.

The Elder Orphan Facebook group is an online community for solo agers, and it has provided me and thousands of others with tremendous value. We connect, share ideas, impart resources, and discover solutions to the problems each face—and we do it together. Members are very willing to help. When members join, suddenly they are not alone and feel isolated in the journey.

In community, members learn a lot from one another. Like in the Facebook group, the members are in different stages. Some people are way ahead and have established sound habits and lifestyles while others follow behind. A mix of different issues certainly challenges each person to grow and see things differently. Group interaction teaches empathy, and provides the opportunity to help those lagging. They enjoy mentorship from members who have achieved a satisfying position. Many times just interacting helps someone reach a goal or find a solution. Each member gets inspired by everyone around them which encourages perseverance.

Evaluate if the group is right for you

Participating in a support group can be uplifting, encouraging, and helpful, but some groups are not for everyone. If a support group is helping you after a few weeks (or months), keep it up. But, if you're on the fence about whether it's helping or not, then reconsider. Ask yourself: "How do I feel? Am I feeling better?" If yes, then the group is worthwhile. If not, either stay for a while longer or find another one.

- What has changed in my life since joining the group? Am I coping better? Am I handling the stress more effectively? What is it like to participate?

- A support group should offer support. Do I feel supported by the members? Can I relate to their worries and concerns?

- Ask yourself, Does the community inspire me to take the appropriate action steps for improving my life? Do I feel safe in the group and free to express myself?

Find Support Group Resources in the Chapter Smart Resources.

Willingness to help others

Since the mid-eighties, scientists have studied a phenomenon called "helper's high." It consists of positive emotions following the selfless service of generosity. Greater health and increased longevity are associated with this state. Acts of helping others releases endorphins which improves mood and boosts self-esteem. It's possible that helping others does more for the happiness of the person helping than the person who receives.

Benefits of giving support

- Helping others isn't a one way street—it builds strong connections with friends and community. When touching another's life in a positive way, you feel connected to them; it's a bonding experience. It builds trust through cooperation which not only brings them closer to you, it brings you closer to them.

- Helping others doesn't add more stress to life, it manages it. By seeing the challenges of others, you can take that point of view into your own. Plus, it makes you more accepting of the stress and hardships all of us face.

- Humans are hardwired for interactions which include touching, eye contact and smiles. These types of interactions release a hormone called Oxytocin which increases bonding and caring for others. And doing good makes us happier which makes us healthier.

- A meaningful life is found through our actions. And it starts with looking for ways to help others. Carol Ryff, a psychologist, reviewed the writings of numerous philosophers and thinkers and found that helping others is "a central feature of a positive, well-lived life."

Ask yourself, Am I willing to share, to convince, to be generous or to invest time in others? Do I try to understand other people's feelings by imagining how things look from their perspective? When upset with someone, do I put myself in their shoes? When in a group setting, are my decisions based on what's fair and just for all? Have I ever taken advantage of people? Does it make sense to be careful how I respond to others especially when feeling miserable or sick? Do I help people equally? Am I addicted to the feeling I receive from the act of giving? When I'm not helping others, do I feel anxious or aimless? Do I feel insecure when someone I help questions or doesn't take my advice? Do I fish for praise after giving advice, or need the other person to acknowledge that I was helpful? Do I feel taken advantage of, like I've made a sacrifice, after a stressful period of helping?

Find Willingness to Help Resources in the Chapter Smart Resources

Find Comfort in Connections

Life's biggest lessons and opportunities are found in connections. Flying solo makes it easy to think I have everything under control because no one is around to challenge me. Friendships and relationships require work—to give and to receive. And it's through connections to others that I find the biggest gifts. Deepen your relationships using these tips.

Smile—one of the simplest ways to connect. Whether it's a brief, cheerful one offered to a perfect stranger, or a tender smile toward a loved one, it's an easy way to deepen relations.

Eye Contact—a powerful way to connect further. The eyes are the gateway to the soul and in today's world, people feel invisible and unrecognized. Eye contact cultivates a level of trust and safety that allows another to open up.

Quality Time—schedule meeting up with a friend, a neighbor, and quiet time with yourself. Making time to connect shifts the quality of relationships. Carving time for self will shift how you relate with others.

Listen with the Heart—really listen to what they say. Avoid listening while formulating a response. Ask yourself: Do you have a tendency to finish their sentences or to interrupt them with my own experiences? Am I listening to my internal dialogue and making assumptions or judgments about this person? Listen from your heart—not the head and be fully present. It will deepen the level of trust and connection.

Do things for—and with—people. Offer a nourishing meal, practice random acts of kindness, tell a joke, offer a hand, or just be there for someone.

Communicate effectively—show up in the conversation and have an open dialogue.

Be Present—ask people about their lives. Then listen. Refrain from checking the phone, glancing at passersby, and other mindless distractions. How you interact affects the energy of the relationship.

Be Authentic—don't masquerade or pretend to be someone you aren't. **Be vulnerable.** Share yourself, and provide a safe place for others to express themselves.

Build Your Own Support Team

Make a list of people who are willing to join a group and to contribute to its success. Family, church members, neighbors, friends, volunteers, caregiver consultants, social workers, counselors, therapists, adult day program staff, home care providers and medical organizations.

Have a support group meeting to evaluate every member's needs, their situation and discuss concerns. Each member has a skill or ability to contribute. Discuss which member is best equipped to handle specific needs. For example, financial skills can assist with monetary guidance, and legal skills provide expertise in legal matters such as wills, health care directives and estate planning. Others may have organizational skills, home repair experience or personal care assistance. Longer distance members can make phone calls, do research, and send emails or reminders. All members should be urged to contribute what each is capable of giving.

Do not assume that everyone is comfortable with and responsible for giving personal care, cleaning or handling finances. Each person is encouraged to bring their own skill or expertise to the group. Pool your resources and agree on a plan of care when a member needs it. Track the time that each person gives—which keeps an even playing field.

Invite professionals to give advice and tips—seek the support and skills from those with experience. A physician and staff will offer guidance and local resources. Pharmacists can answer questions regarding medications and interactions. Clergy and church members can offer spiritual guidance and assistance with occasional meals or transportation. Home care agencies offer certified and licensed staff to provide custodial and skilled care services. Medical organizations that address Parkinson's disease, Alzheimer's disease, cancer, etc., should also be contacted for information and support groups.

Those living alone cannot procrastinate to create a community of helping hands. Nearly three-fourths of middle-income Boomers have not planned for their retirement care. Only one in five have a rough plan for how they will receive care in retirement; just 8% have a detailed plan.

Social Connectedness Goals:

- Develop healthy social connections throughout life to prevent disease, disability, injury and premature death and assure a high quality of life.
- Achieve equity in the opportunity to form and maintain healthy individual, family, and community-level social connections.
- Provide opportunities for safe, healthy and productive social interactions in neighborhoods and communities.
- Promote strong, healthy social connections across all life stages to support healthy development and healthy behaviors.

SMART PURPOSE

Life purpose consists of embracing your central motivating aims— the reasons for getting up in the morning. Purpose can guide life decisions, influence behavior, shape goals, offer a sense of direction, and create meaning. For some, purpose is connected to vocation— meaningful work. For others, purpose lies in the commitments to family or friends. While a few seek meaning through spirituality or religious beliefs. And partly, people may find purpose in all of these.

Purpose is unique; what you identify as your path may be different from others. Furthermore, your purpose can shift and change throughout life in response to the evolving priorities and fluctuations of the experiences. Purpose doesn't always surround a vocation, nor does it mean having a mission to change the world. It can be simple— you know that your contribution will make a positive impact on your life and on those around you.

Ask yourself? What makes you feel useful? Is there a "what's next," an inner calling or a bright idea that gets your blood racing?

Purpose and Passion

Personal-growth expert, Jennifer Louden, author, Why Bother, encourages us to discover the desire for what's next by asking that exact question because it opens the mind to..I wonder.. and What if? When asked each morning upon awakening, Why Bother, extends a chance to open the mind, heart, and to spark new life. Louden tells us by asking the question, it can bring you to a place of increased vitality, true satisfaction, and deeper meaning. Through reflection and stories from others, Louden shows that asking the question reveals that your life is worth the effort even after sidelining the dreams to raise kids, pay the rent, or taking care of aging parents.

Once you tap into the deep desires, you're set to move forward— even when the world seems in dire straits. After all, no one wants the alternative—giving up, shutting down, or calling it over. Louden encourages us to, Get your bother on.

Why should it matter to get your bother on? To have a sense of purpose—a reason to keep moving forward? Having purpose won't remove the heartache or disappointment one has experienced, but it will unfasten a calling that's been buried or ignored for many years or perhaps an entire life. Having a sense of purpose, a reason to get out of bed and make life better shifts a rigid perspective into a receptive one.

It was family caregiving that triggered bother within me, in good and irritating ways as you read in Chapter 1. It was the nemesis that transitioned self-involvement into more meaning. I learned selflessness through the act of helping. Is there a challenge or situational hardship that provoked annoyance within you, something that stirred a bee in your bonnet? It could simply be an irritation or worry. However, it may be something else. A burning desire for more, perhaps?

The truth about purpose. We're on this planet for a period of time. During that span we do things. Some are important and some are not. But the important things give our life meaning and if we're lucky, we reap a deep sense of satisfaction. So instead of thinking that life's purpose is an earthshaking end-all, ponder instead, What can I do with my time that gives a sense of meaning?

Viktor Frankl encourages his readers in Man's Search for Meaning, to strive for reasons to live no matter the hardship. Readers learn Frankl's beliefs that sustain the desire to live even under the most inhumane and desperate situations. In the concentration camps in Nazi Germany, he found his purpose for survival. For Frankl, it was his strong desire to reunite with his wife, to write the book, Man's Search for Meaning, and in spite of suffering and hopelessness, Frankl discovered meaning. Read more articles about Purpose and Passion in the Chapter Smart Resources

Reflect Upon Life's Purpose

When are you in flow? When in the flow, you are so fully engaged and immersed in an activity that you feel relaxed, but also challenged, interested but not stressed. When in the flow, you lose your sense of time, and you focus only on the task at hand. Ask yourself: What types of activities bring me to this place? Are there parts of a job, or a volunteer organization that makes me feel the time speed by? Are there hobbies that seem to make a day disappear? Who do I spend time with who helps me forget my worries, get rid of past baggage and future concerns, and just be? These clues can help fine-tune what resonates with you most deeply in life.

Life Meaning

To hear Jim Isenberg talk about his multiple careers and now his volunteer projects, he could inspire the dead. What that told me—Jim's passion flows through him. Isenberg is the co-founder of Grandpas United in White Plains NY, an intergenerational youth mentoring program. He is the retired executive director of the New York Region of the North American Family Institute where he directed the development of innovative, community-based programs serving youth and families. What stood out was his natural ability to initiate change and to make an astounding impact in lives, for older volunteers as well as the younger generations. When talking to Jim, I could hardly keep up with the conversation. Jim had all sorts of recommendations for problems. A real visionary.

Most of us aren't high achievers like Jim. But we don't have to be a go-getter to have meaning. Nancy, a retired English teacher, was hired to run her community's local public library. I've seen her in action. She has a natural, easy way of stimulating creativity in people, especially students. It's stunning to watch. When working on projects with kids and older students, her spirit lights up the room. And those who observe are mesmerized. Nancy can generate ideas, using her quick wit and colorful terms, and like magic the kids jump up to volunteer, grab art supplies, and run off to start a project. Like Jim, Nancy has an innate sense of inspiring young people. When I was talking to both, I struggled to keep up. They are unique and inventive—and they have discovered passion after their main careers were over.

Whose faces do you see when you think about love? A sense of meaning or purpose is intrinsically tied to other people. Or perhaps it's not but certain animals that you feel a most profound connection with.

What does "love" mean to you? Or perhaps it is both professional and personal: the organization you work for, or the people you volunteer to help, or the community or cause you have come to believe in. Love can mean many things to many people, but when you imagine what it means to you, it can often point you in the right direction in a sense of purpose: thinking about the reason that you are on this Earth, and the legacy you want to leave behind.

Edith, a retired flight attendant, lives in my high rise. I don't know her well, but she's a reliable pet-sitter, dog-walker, duck-feeder, and cat-carer. Outside, she's never alone; an animal is always with her. One day I overheard her say, "I'm the luckiest person, because of all the pets who love me." Every pet in the building certainly does, and even the ones outside—when Texas got unseasonably cold (below twenty degrees for six consecutive days,) Edith was spotted feeding the ducks across the street and even carried a near frozen duck home to thaw. "What are you going to do with that duck?" I asked when seeing her in the lobby. She had a plan. "I'm putting it in a warm tub of water." And she did. Five days later she carried the duck, defrosted and healthy, back to its home across the street. Edith has found her purpose.

Anne was an art therapist who worked in a variety of settings, including a school for kids with Down's Syndrome, a psychiatric hospital for acute short term inpatients, a nursing home, and a small rest home for residents with psychiatric disorders and substance abusers. The patients became "her children" as she worked with them for twenty-three years. Most of her patients had no family. At the same time, she cared for her mother. Eventually, stress and chronic health forced Anne to retire at age sixty-two. Then her mother passed away. Did Anne fade into retirement? No—she volunteered at the local animal shelter. When her chronic pain got too much for her to help the animals, she found an online volunteer position at the Cornell Lab of Ornithology. These volunteers operate remote cameras in various locations, including Kauai, Montana, and Texas, watching and recording birds, and tweeting information about them. Anne loved the work and stayed there for five years.

Never give up was Anne's motto. Inspired by her father to accept life on its terms, she found ways to adapt to each situation she found herself in and keep going, to search out new interests. She is a good example of someone who adjusts her roadmap to suit the realities of aging. Now she studies herbalism and takes online courses, engaging and challenging her intellect.

What are you most willing to put effort into? We all have different levels of motivation for different tasks, and some activities feel almost effortless because we like doing them so much. So, think about when you actually enjoy hard work. Paradoxically, of course, those activities likely don't feel much like work—at least not in the same way as doing activities that you don't enjoy doing. It brings to mind the old saying, "Find something you love to do, and you'll never work a day in your life." Of course, many of us will never truly love our jobs, and that's okay. And even those of us who have been able to feel passionate about our work may go through many periods of feeling taxed, stressed, and overworked by those same careers. But if you can examine your patterns about the things in life that you worked hard for, it will help you determine what type of pursuits are most worthy of your time—and your heart and soul.

Debra Hallisey is the founder of Advocate for Mom and Dad. Like me, she discovered her passion after caring for her mother after her father died. At age fifty-eight, a few months into her caregiving, she lost her job and discovered how much of her identity was tied to her work. Debra told me, "I always enjoyed writing, but never pursued it because I didn't get good grades in grammar. My style of writing did not fit the mold for high school and honestly grammar and punctuation are not my strong suit. But as an adult, I realized that I'm not trying to get a good grade, I'm trying to share my caregiving story and empower other family caregivers. I can hire an editor to clean up my commas."

Debra is now in her sixties and has found her voice. Writing and speaking on caregiving issues, she works with family caregivers. She finds this calling much more satisfying than her previous career. She started the business as a leap of faith and trusted that this is what she was meant to do. She told me that a long time ago she read the book Do What You Love and The Money Will Follow. It stuck with her and has been a touchstone as she's worked on her business. It hasn't been easy, but she self-funded the business with retirement money and then reached a point where she could pull a small salary.

If you were to write your own obituary, what would you include? As much as this feels morbid, or even silly, imagine what you want your life's legacy to be. The exercise can be helpful when searching for purpose. Looking back on life as if one nears its end can truly be useful in determining what to devote precious time—in future moments, months, years, and decades—to doing. Those who work in hospice say they hear the same regrets from patients; they get caught up in worrying about the things that shouldn't have mattered. What do you want to leave behind—tangibly, emotionally, and socially? And how would you have wanted someone to be able to summarize the years you spent on this planet?

Gee Kin Chou had a twenty-five-year career in business, followed by twenty years in public education. Born in China to parents with no formal education, Gee Kin understood the immigrant experience and the daunting maze of challenges they face in an unfamiliar country. So he co founded The Boombox Collaboratory, a nonprofit that enables working Americans to use their personal contacts to help immigrant students and others to broaden their career horizons. To address the persistent inequity inherent in this "opportunity gap," Boombox harnesses a valuable asset that many older Americans overlook—their social and professional network. Chou has leveled the playing field and provides every student a fair start in life.

If you had a bonus day—free of all responsibilities, appointments, and commitments, and you were fully rested and recharged and could do anything you wanted for 12 hours—what would you do? I know, I know. In this age of busyness, a status symbol, no one can even imagine a day with no responsibilities, especially a day when one is fully rested. But just try, for a moment, to picture a completely blank slate—free of concerns. Imagine you're recharged with energies and talents ready to spend on anything you choose. What would you devote your energies to?

Michael Krieger was never a caregiver for his family, but he enjoyed sharing time with his grandparents. He wrote and recorded original songs and held concerts, primarily in restaurants, and at one event, a woman invited him to perform for the residents of her senior housing community. I want you to play everything you're playing here, she told him. Michael did and the gig lasted for over twenty years. When a family thanks him for helping their loved one, Michael jokes, "Oh, I thought they were helping me." He is lifted by the work he does. Over the years, he has encouraged the residents to keep digging for ways to gain passion and to give to others. Michael's dream of playing music as a career did come true, though not in the way he thought it would. When he started singing for older adults, he knew very quickly that he had found his niche. He saw the impact his music was having in their lives and it never felt like work to him.

Legacy does not always carry a bag of medals and trophies, a big paycheck, or a trust fund. Leaving the world a better place or inspiring another is far more significant than making a lot of money. Maybe you've developed a strong guidance system that directed you in life from where you were to where you wanted to go. Children, high school students, and young adults all have the need for guidance. If you're one with a strong GPS, then you have what it takes to mentor. Many younger people have lost their way and need strong mentors to teach them skills.

Mentoring Skills

Even older adults need help developing internal guidance, especially for those challenged in health literacy. Managing chronic disease is very complex, and the cognitive and sensory changes associated with aging compound the challenges. If you have a strong GPS system, you have an opportunity to bring about positive health behavior changes. The following list describes the skills adults need when challenged with aging.

Communication: Understand what others are saying and feeling and also convey your own ideas and feelings. Effective communication skills enable you and those you mentor to build trust, engage, resolve problems, gain clarity and direction, and create better relationships. Relationship: Verbal and nonverbal behaviors and responses to interactions with others affect people's ability to make associations and make impressions on others in social situations. Whether it is a brief encounter or a long-term friendship, focusing on these skills make interaction more productive. Relationship abilities encourage personal growth, support, team building, and add more pleasure to one's life.

Organization: Good organization skills can save time, prevent miscommunications and improve efficiency. These abilities, no matter the age, help you plan, prioritize, and achieve your goals, which, in turn, can improve how well you age.

Problem-solving: Good problem-solvers remain calm when they encounter obstacles and assess their options for solutions—which is needed for aging well alone. Problem-solving gives you a mechanism for identifying these things, figuring out why they are broken and determining a course of action to fix them.

Self-confidence: Believing in yourself, your abilities, actions and decisions. If you have confidence in yourself, you are more inclined to pursue ambitious goals, try new things, and believe you can succeed. Older adults have a great need to learn self-reliance since so many live without help at home.

Adaptability: People who handle change well adjust quickly and easily to new situations, get along with a variety of personalities, and thrive in any environment. They remain calm in startling and challenging situations. Adaptability is a soft skill that enables you to quickly pick up new behaviors and responses to changing circumstances.

Integrity: Integrity means doing what is right and telling the truth. Having integrity means that you live in accordance with your deepest values, and you always keep their word—to others and to yourself. Richard Leider, a nationally-ranked coach and purpose expert, says that "genuine purpose points to the end of a self-absorbed, self-serving life." When your authentic purpose becomes clear, you will be able to share it with the whole world.

Special Desire

Does a special dream filled with passion live within? How much time are you devoting to it? If you're not devoting time every single day you're not contributing to its fruition. It's fairly easy to predict whether you'll achieve that dream or not. The same principle can be applied to your relationships, your kids, your exercise regime, your general level of happiness, your political standing, and so on, into every life aspect. How much of your day is spent doing what you want? How many hours of the week are you devoting to mastering the thing you're most passionate about? How many hours each day do you waste?

Greatest Joy

Let's conduct a joy review. Set aside a half hour or so and make a list of the times you've felt the greatest joy. Think broadly. You'll be amazed at what comes back to you. The times can involve people or just you. For example, the first time I did the review, I recalled teaching a group of adults, presenting them with a plan for the future. Then I remembered the time I created an art collage of my childhood photos, another when I was in a retreat at Esalen, and when I was traveling back with my cat from California to Texas to help my parents. Joy can come from anywhere at the most unexpected times, but reviewing those moments can help you find joy in the present and in the days to come. It's all part of finding your purpose and passion—knowing what brings you joy can help align your internal guidance system and determine your life purpose.

John, the retired IT professional summed it up well: "When seeking your absolute passion, just bring an everything is possible attitude with you. Even when something you've tried doesn't fit, learn from the experience and keep it on the table. Carry the thought while searching and know there is a definite purpose out there. The satisfaction gaining it will far outweigh the blood, sweat, and tears. If you make just one moment better for another, you have done all God has intended! What better report card could you have?"

SMART FAITH | SPIRITUALITY

Why is faith important and why having it matters? Faith isn't a conviction to hold onto in tough times; faith is a living presence that anchors within and illuminates our pathway in times of darkness, giving strength in times of weakness. More remarkably, it's a living spirit inspired by God to prepare and equip us to do good works. Faith is God in action.

What does faith and spirituality mean to you? Does faith sustain and give you strength? Are there certain beliefs that you practice? Have the practices developed self-trust or trust in God? Has life become restful and peaceful by faith? What have you gained? Reflecting upon the past trials and challenges, list the things that God resolved? The kind you had little influence because the problem was too complicated, and only God could have remedied. Journal about what you have learned and the miracles you've seen. Contemplate upon these questions for insights. As life throws stumbling blocks, draw on the epiphanies and reminders for inspiration and strength.

For me, religion is irrelevant. It's trust and faith in God. Prior to the pandemic, I was a New Age believer—all individuals must focus on an ultimate goal of developing the god-aspect within. The aim is to develop the self and bring it into awareness of its nature as divine. When COVID happened, the world turned inside out. I lost the internal compass and became disoriented. People feared dying which drove panic. That fear lapsed into chronic anxiety; ultimately infusing terror and imminent doom. This level of fear affected everyone's sense of normality.

Staying isolated and spending time alone in 2020 was a blessing and I leaned on the God of my youth, not the New Age principles. I realized over the thirty-eight years of practice, they failed to bring peace and tranquility, especially along imminent danger. From this, I have gained the true meaning of responsibility, to be respectful and be righteous. That's when the Living Spirit settled within.

Spiritual practice is different for people. Some practice Christianity, Judaism, Islam, New Age, and some don't have faith beyond the self. Our journeys vary. My choice is Christ centered—to rely on His goodness as the foundation. To trust in His provision—for all that I do, do it for His glory. That's my faith. What about you? If spiritual belief and practice are important, each of us deserve the confidence to share that part with those who care about us. Even for those who don't believe in a Supreme God, they deserve to be heard.

The point of the Faith | Spirituality domain is to discover how satisfied you are with it. Relying on something grander than ourselves has the power to carry us through the arduous times. Growing older has many challenges and by faith in God, a Being larger and more powerful than ourselves to assist and help, will give confidence and strength. If not, this stage has the potential to put an older person in a precarious position.

Assess Your Spiritual Journey

How did the Faith | Spirituality domain rank? If below 5, consider building a more faithful and spiritual practice. In doing so, the years ahead could be filled with inner strength and rest. And heaven knows as people grow older, we need a lot.

A Gallup poll reports close to 90 percent of adults in the U.S. believe in God or a universal spirit. The majority of people pray often, with 75 percent praying at least sometimes. And about the same number of Americans think the U.S. would be better off if more people were religious. And yet, most rarely talk about spiritual experiences or our relationship with God. But we tend to argue about the facts as we see them, and avoid revealing anything about our deepest personal convictions.

However, there are exceptions. Some are willing to share their spiritual and religious beliefs. They're happy to tell us about what God is doing to help them, or how Jesus saved them from addiction. But these are few and far between. We're uncomfortable, so the conversation shuts down. Do you share your faith with others? How confident are you when doing so? Here are a few factors that make people reluctant—even if the beliefs and experiences are profoundly important. Review below and think about your reasons:

Is religion, spirituality, God, Jesus Christ, the Bible, Torah a taboo topic? Do you avoid it like politics? Each generates a lot of disruption when we don't see eye-to-eye and we fear fallout or push back. Yet, the topic is important, so let's dig deeper and distinguish between different ways of talking about it. Attempts to convert someone to our belief system will create friction. But an honest discussion about our personal experiences are different, and harder to argue. "I felt such peace once I studied the Bible," feels a lot different from, "You must obey The Bible or you will go to Hades." The former captures an experience; the latter is a statement of belief.

Ask yourself: "Do I honor my personal experiences of faith in God?" If yes, how so? Make a list of the things or ways God and faith has changed your life for the better. Are you worried that you will say something offensive, insensitive, or politically incorrect if you speak your truth?

Generally, people are not offended by others' beliefs, provided they don't infringe on their own freedoms. Also, saying I felt God's unconditional love is less likely to offend than saying God wants you to convert to a certain religion or to vote for a particular candidate.

Ask yourself: How willing am I to share my spiritual experiences with others? And when sharing my experiences, do I want the other person to feel guilty or feel wrong about their belief? Do I convey a sense of righteousness when sharing my truth? Are you afraid of being the odd-person out?

It's easy to think we'll be the weird one, the outlier, if we broach a taboo subject. We don't want to be seen as a religious nut. The irony is that the things people avoid talking about are ones that most people have had.

Ask yourself: Have I developed an open mindset, like the one Dr. Seuss promotes? "Do what you want to do, say what you want to say, because those who matter don't mind, and those who do mind don't matter." Have I embraced a mindset that fosters giving rather than taking? Do I seek comfort over resolution? Do I seek guidance from those wiser than me?

Are you concerned and afraid that you'll be seen as foolish if you speak honestly about believing in God? People often believe there's a negative parallel between being religious and being intelligent. In reality, knowing someone's religious beliefs tells us nothing about how smart they are.

Did you know that Sir Isaac Newton was a man of God? Many intelligent people are religious or have strong spiritual convictions. And while some may assume that believing in God makes you a dumb person, most people don't make that assumption because they don't want to be sanctimonious and self-righteous.

Ask yourself: When afraid of being myself and wholly expressing my spiritual beliefs, who am I putting my trust in, myself or God? How much time do I spend in prayer and in the quietness?

Try not to focus on the fear. Choose to dwell on something better—joy. To focus on fear creates more fear; to focus on the One who takes fear away is to find solace. Choose to fix your thoughts on what is true, honorable, right, pure, lovely, and admirable.

Does speaking about faith feel like a weakness? At the heart of that is fear of vulnerability. When we share our deepest feelings, experiences, and beliefs we take a big risk. Like saying "I need help," it shows emotional vulnerability. But when we take that risk, we're being honest and open to intimacy which requires trust. Consider instead: Maybe if I would allow feeling vulnerable with others, there would be fewer arguments about religion and politics, especially, if we shared from the heart.

Ask yourself: What am I afraid will happen if I share my faith? What family and friends can I begin to have spiritual conversations with? People who change the world are people with conviction. Spend time in prayer, asking God to help you become a person of conviction who values the things He values.

Conversation starters: What single thing would you like to make absolutely certain you do (if at all possible) during your lifetime? How are you growing personally? What do you think would probably surprise most people about you? Why? What is your greatest strength, and what are you doing to develop it? What single thing would you like to make absolutely certain you do (if possible) during your lifetime? What are 2 or 3 major truths upon which you have based your decision-making? In your opinion, who was/is Jesus Christ? Get more questions in the Faith | Spirituality Resources in the next chapter.

Are you a bystander? Since others aren't talking about God or spirituality, you choose the same because you don't want to look weak? People aren't talking about God, faith, etc.—so I shouldn't either. But when you lead the way, others become more receptive.

At a Christmas luncheon a friend hosted, I raised the topic of studying the Bible. The subject came up naturally and I went with it. I always assumed people would rather chew nails than talk about God and the Bible, or have a strong opposition to it. The discussion was engaging. I learned things about the guests that I wouldn't have guessed, and felt more connected with them at the end of the day.

To overcome passive behaviors, ask yourself: Do I express my needs clearly and directly? Are my feelings expressed inappropriately? Do I show respect for other people? In my conversations, are many 'I statements' used? Do I listen to others without interrupting them? Do I speak calmly and clearly? Do I ask for what I want? Do I stand up for myself? Do I allow others to make their own decisions and speak up for themselves?

Spiritual Practices

I am a follower of Jesus Christ, maybe you are, maybe you're not. When practicing the following activities, edit for your preferences.

1. Do you practice quiet time and look forward to that time spent in faith? For me it's with Christ.
2. When making choices, do you seek guidance first?
3. What motivates your relationship with Christ or God? Is it love or duty?
4. Make a list of the life changes as a result of your worship experiences.
5. When God makes you aware of His specific will in an area of your life—do you follow the prompt?
6. Do you demonstrate a life of your choosing or a life directed by God?
7. Focus on peace, contentment, and joy to characterize your life rather than worry and anxiety.
8. Do you trust that God will help you through any problem or crisis?
9. How much confidence do you have that your faith will see it through?

Pray in Faith

1. In prayer, focus on discovering God's will more than expressing your needs.

2. Trust God to answer when you pray and wait patiently on His timing.

3. Always include thanksgiving, praise, confession, and requests in prayers.

4. Expect growth in your prayer life and intentionally seek help to improve.

5. Spend as much time listening to God as talking to Him.

6. Pray because you have complete dependence on your faith for everything.

7. Participate regularly in group prayer.

8. Maintain an attitude of prayer throughout each day.

9. Believe your prayers impact your life and the lives of others.

10. Engage in prayer time.

Be in Fellowship with Believers

1. Forgive others when their actions harm you.

2. Admit your errors in relationships and humbly seek forgiveness from the one you've hurt.

3. Allow other Followers to hold you accountable for spiritual growth.

4. Seek to live in harmony with other members of your family.

5. Place the interest of others above your self-interest.

6. Be gentle and kind in your interactions with others.

7. Encourage and listen to feedback from others to help you discover areas for relationship growth.

8. Show patience in relationships with family and friends.

9. Encourage others by pointing out their strengths rather than criticizing their weaknesses.

10. Honoring time commitments demonstrates that you value relationships over work/career/hobbies.

Minister to Others

1. Know your spiritual gifts and use them to serve others.

2. Serve others expecting nothing in return.

3. Extend yourself and show respect to people you meet.

4. Meeting the needs of others provides a sense of purpose.

5. Share biblical truth with those you serve as God gives opportunity.

6. Act as if other's needs are as important as your own

7. Expect God to use you every day in His work.

8. Contribute time to ministry.

9. Help others identify their gifts and become involved in ministry.

Spiritual growth is not easy. We must work at it. Today. Tomorrow. Always. But we can take comfort in knowing that "Spiritual Growth Is A Choice."

The Spiritual Person

Few spiritual traits which result from trusting God:

- God-centered. For me it's Christ-centered and to follow the Bible.
- Empowered by the Holy Spirit.
- Introduces others to faith.
- Effective prayer life.
- Trusts and obeys God.
- Experiences love, joy, peace, patience, kindness, faithfulness, gentleness, goodness and self-control.

In Eastern Meditation, the goal is to empty one's mind with the intention to connect with the essential nature. Christian Mediation has the goal of filling one's mind with Scripture, with the intention to connect with God[3]. In Judaism, the goal is to heighten one's understanding of the Torah, understand the ritual and religious observances, and give direction to prayer. In Islam, the goal is to remember God, the Sustainer, Creator, and Caretaker of all existence.

SMART TRANSPORTATION | MOBILITY

My lifestyle promotes walking for a lot of my needs. Public transit is convenient, but walking is my sweet spot. The lifestyle that was designed with intention. It delivers the resources for good health, close proximity to shopping and entertainment with little need for a car. I never swayed from or second guessed that preference. That goal put me in an urban area that's relatively flat, and foot or bike friendly. Austin was another place I lived. I used a bicycle or walked a lot there as well, and that is not a flat city! No matter the terrain, feet over a car is the best therapy for aging well.

My main reasons for walking:

1. Healthful
2. Saves time
3. Less costly
4. Outdoor delight
5. Lessens carbon footprint
6. Amusing
7. Serene
8. Enhances stability
9. Burns fat
10. Elevates immunity

How many times this week did you use a car? Could you have walked instead? Although walking may take longer, consider the benefits. Perhaps driving does save time but walking would improve health and even your balance; both are chief factors for better aging. According to the Mayo Clinic, walking helps a person get fit, lowers blood pressure, maintains good cholesterol levels and generally enhances one's mood.

Evaluate Transportation

Appraising mobility, deciding where driving is critical. For example, when living in Austin, I experienced two walkable lifestyles. One was downtown—the other was centrally located. Both had brief demands for a car. If you want to be car independent, live in an area where amenities exist within a 2 mile radius of work, hobbies, shopping, medical facilities, entertainment, libraries, bank, and food because you will save precious energy compared to commuting. Of course, it's not always possible to walk. I picked a distance of 5 miles for close proximity. Driving is faster than everything else, but wait... depending on traffic, walking could be faster than public transportation or driving a car. I do not walk to services that are 5 miles away. Two is the most I can handle. However a 5 mile marker allows for less hectic traffic if driving.

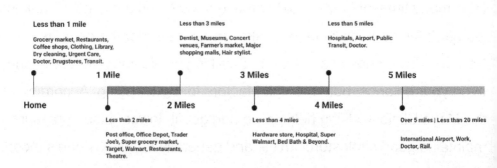

List My Transportation Needs | Destinations

Less than 1 mile
Grocery market, Restaurants, Coffee shops, Clothing, Library, Dry cleaning, Urgent Care, Doctor, Drugstores, Transit.

Less than 3 miles
Dentist, Museums, Concert venues, Farmer's market, Major shopping malls, Hair stylist.

Less than 5 miles
Hospitals, Airport, Public Transit, Doctor.

1 Mile   3 Miles   5 Miles

Home   2 Miles   4 Miles

Less than 2 miles
Post office, Office Depot, Trader Joe's, Super grocery market, Target, Walmart, Restaurants, Theatre.

Less than 4 miles
Hardware store, Hospital, Super Walmart, Bed Bath & Beyond.

Over 5 miles | Less than 20 miles
International Airport, Work, Doctor, Rail.

Healthiest modes of transportation

Choosing a mode of transportation that enables physical exercise is always preferred to those that do not, when good health is the goal. CDC recommends for those 60 years of age or older, who are generally fit with no limiting health conditions, to do 150 minutes 5 days a week of moderate intensity exercise. Guess what brisk walking is? Moderate intensity exercise. For even greater health benefits, go beyond 300 minutes a week of moderate-intensity activity (60 minutes a day, 5 days a week.) Of course, biking or running is more intense.

Biking

There are times when walking won't cut it, perhaps because the destination is too far, or because you're in a rush. In these situations, consider biking instead of driving. Bikes are much cheaper to buy and to maintain over a car, and they don't require much space. Although walking is more energy-efficient than driving, biking is even better. Some say that biking is 50 times more efficient than driving, and that the bike is one of the most energy-efficient modes of mobility. Bikes don't add to the carbon footprint.

What's your need for a car?

Having a car gives freedom—to go wherever you want, when you want. Pick a destination, grab the keys, hop in the car, and you're off. If that's the goal, keep it. But there are better reasons for not having one or at least for using it less. Cars are costly to buy and maintain. They break down, need new tires, gas, oil changes, and this maintenance requires time, attention, and money. If you're objective, options for movability will be discovered.

- Walk
- Get a ride with a friend or neighbor
- Use public transportation—bus, train, subway, and trolley
- Taxicabs
- Rent a car
- Bicycle
- In-line skates
- Scooters
- Buses, trains and airplanes for longer trips

Creative ways to get to around

Start your own shared ride program with local connections. You've heard of housing services like Airbnb and ride-sharing services such as Uber and Lyft which help homeowners and car owners to rent out rooms and car seats. There's just one thing wrong with the sharing economy—there's no sharing. Rooms and rides come at a cost. What these services really do is make it easy for buyers and sellers of spare rooms and rides to find each other and make a transaction.

The Internet and smartphones have made another kind of sharing possible—real sharing. Ride sharing is an eco-friendly way of commuting by sharing your car with others. If you're interested in ride sharing, to find rides or share your car within your personal network, check these apps out.

- Uber is by far the most popular ride sharing service
- Lyft, the second-largest ride sharing app by volume
- Curb is the #1 taxi app in the US that connects you to fast, convenient and safe rides across the U.S.
- Wingz provides transportation to and from airports. Now, they offer around-town rides in a few, select cities. Riders can pick and choose their favorite drivers, and the company promises that moving forward, the service will remain less expensive than a taxi or limo.
- Via app uses a "logistics engine" to fill as many seats as possible in cars headed toward popular destinations. Unlike Uber and Lyft, the routes are static—just tell the service where you'd like to go and you'll get dropped off at a nearby location.
- Scoop is a ride sharing app for iOS and Android that lets you arrange carpooling with your co-workers and neighbors.
- Arro taps into a database of more than 20,000 licensed taxis to provide clients with on-demand transportation. Unfortunately, at this time Arro is only available in a select group of cities, but if you happen to live in New York City, Boston, Miami, and Houston you can take advantage of the services.

- BlaBlaCar, BlaBlaCarpool, and bus service are some of the best in recent times. Addressing the problem of rising traffic and gas prices, BlaBlaCar offers a great deal to all of its users. You can pool with other vehicles or passengers covering your common routes. Find a carpool, or if you have a car, you can find people who can travel with you and share expenses.

- Waze Carpool is a great app for doing daily travel. Via helps you make the most out of your time and helps you travel faster by getting quick rides to your destination. The app offers an easy to use interface and quick response time.

- Karpoolclub app can help you to find your favorite groups to share a ride. A better utilization of your car, van and trusted network to help share your ride for kids, adults, seniors and even pets.

- RideConnect.com is a ride sharing platform with which you can create your own ride share. Develop a ride share program with neighbors, friends, and family.

Become a Better Driver

If you must drive, polish your skills. It's a good idea to evaluate and strengthen your driving abilities.

- Check in periodically with family and friends to see if they have any concerns about your driving safety or if they noticed changes.

- Get regular eye exams and health check-ups to confirm that you have no underlying conditions that could impair operating a car.
- Get an evaluation by a driving specialist and take a refresher course if needed.

Find a Roadmap for Transportation Independence in the Smart Resources.

Ask yourself? Do I have concerns about my driving?

- on the freeway because my reaction time is slower?
- after dark because my night vision has worsened?
- while making a left turn because I can't judge the distance of oncoming cars?
- difficulty reading street signs and road instructions?

Common physical changes due to age or medical conditions:

- slower reflexes
- weak or unsteady
- trouble walking or carrying objects
- confused about your whereabouts
- seeing clearly or needing new glasses
- taking three or more medications (prescribed or over-the-counter)

Recommendations

- Health issues affect an older adult's driving—see your healthcare provider.

- Check vision, balance, strength and mobility, and look for factors that affect how you react to different driving situations.
- If you're concerned about someone's (or your own) memory problems, dementia, or other issues that affect their ability to think and make decisions—talk to the person's healthcare provider.
- Work with a healthcare provider to identify the issues.

Professional driving evaluation and assistance

If you have concerns about an older adult's or your own driving, get a referral to an occupational therapist (OT) or a driving rehabilitation specialist (DRS).

- An OT can thoroughly review general skills and note areas that need improvement, as well as help make a transportation plan.
- A DRS can evaluate an older adult's driving for safety and for potential benefit from having skills rehabilitated.

Get the Driving Specialist Directory in the Transportation Resources in THE Chapter Smart Resources.

Tips for Driving in Traffic

Remove distractions. In heavy traffic conditions, the road is crowded and the flow is irregular, but avoid getting impatient. Limit distractions:

- Turn off the cell phone or put it on silent mode.
- Switch off the music, or turn the volume down.

- Ask passengers to quieten down until you're free of dense traffic.

Defensive driving covers a wide set of skills—use these for an emergency situation, if another vehicle tries to merge into you.

- Keep scanning traffic and road conditions.
- Identify unsafe vehicles—those erratically merging across lanes, speeding dangerously, or drifting within a lane.
- Follow the flow of traffic.
- Signal before turning or merging into a lane.
- Allow plenty of space between you and other vehicles/ structures.
- Never drive while tired or emotionally agitated.
- Avoid heavy traffic. Leave fifteen or thirty minutes before the start or after the end of rush hour. The worst times for traffic (rush hour) varies where you live. Generally, expect it to be heaviest between 7:30-09:00, and 16:00-18:00.
- Allow a two second distance between you and traffic in front of you. Gauge the seconds of distance between you and the car ahead of you.
- Drive at or 5 mph below the speed limit, even on a highway. It's important to feel safe when behind the wheel. Don't drive too much slower because that makes other drivers around you impatient, leading to dangerous driving situations.

- Prepare for emergency maneuvers.
- Leave the freeway if you feel uncomfortable.

Obtain Community Medical or Health Care Rides

Ask yourself: Are there private or non-profit transportation services? Public transit nearby? Can I walk errands? Do medical/ transportation services exist where I live? Are friends or family available for rides or help with errands? What other transportation options are available?

Unfortunately, many people with healthcare needs can't make it doctor's appointments. Over 3.5 million Americans miss medical appointments or delay getting medical care each year because they can't secure a ride. If that's the case, contact:

- Call your local Area Agency on Aging Department for ride information.
- Call your city government offices for Paratransit rides.
- Go to Ridester.com—Uber's program for health rides—Uber Health.
- Check with your State Health and Human Services Department.
- Check with the Insurance company.
- Check with the doctor's office and health care provider.
- You may be eligible for rides via Medicaid to and from your doctor's office, the hospital, and other medical facilities for

approved care. Consult your state program for help arranging these services.

- Contact GogoGrandparent.com—they schedule rides by phone, no need for a smartphone with an app.

SMART FINANCES | MONEY MATTERS

Possessing money means less worry about covering expenses. Having enough of it will pay for any emergency. When you are financially secure, stress goes down—leaving you free to focus on more gratifying undertakings.

Financial means and security decline with age. Younger seniors may be relatively healthy and able to continue working if needed, the older seniors may need expensive care and have dwindling resources to pay for it. Once past age 75, people see a shift in the other direction. Because there's a huge gap in how people save money so financial resources vary widely. While some are financially secure, able to cover the costs of housing, other necessities, and long-term care if needed, significant numbers of low-, moderate-, and middle-income households live in unaffordable housing and lack assets to cover the costs of home modifications or in-home support.

At 55, my savings and retirement investments were remiss. Like health, I knew having little money would affect my relationships, home, and even health. There's nothing seductive about money when there's not enough of it. I know what it feels like to struggle with rising costs when a paycheck doesn't keep up with inflation, it's exhausting. And when we have more, it offers a sense of security, confidence, and stability.

Tips for Handling Money

- Don't let fear of failing stop you from taking action.
- If you don't have an investment or savings account, open one.
- Live below your means.
- Know where your money is going.
- Create value and make money selling it.
- Think of money as a simple tool like a hammer.
- Every time you make a financial decision, consider how it will affect your wealth in the future.

Planning for an Uncertain Future

Baby Boomers have arrived at the retirement stage and for a vast part they've landed with few resources for paying for the long-term care. The duration and level of long-term care will vary from person to person and often change over time. Here are some statistics (all are "on average") to consider: (Source: LongTermCare.gov)

- Someone turning age 65 today has almost a 70% chance of needing some type of long-term care services and supports in their remaining years

- Women need care longer (3.7 years) than men (2.2 years)
- One-third of today's 65 year-olds may never need long-term care support, but 20 percent will need it for longer than 5 years

The significant portion of the needed assistance will be covered by public programs and some private insurance, but much of the care will be an uninsured private responsibility—one that will be distributed unequally.

My parents did a decent job in long-term planning. They took charge of the legal and financial matters, their funeral expenses, lived affordably, carried no mortgage, paid bills on time, had a thriving social circle, and a strong faith organization. Where they fell short was in personal care, and planning for assistance with the activities of daily living. That fell on their 3 daughters. Maybe they didn't think much assistance would be required since all through life, they're needs were simple. No one wants to think about getting sick, frail, and dependent.

While over a third of those turning 65 are projected to never receive help from family, three out of 10 will rely on family for more than two years of needed care. My parents relied on three daughters for seven years. So, the time one will need depends on the physical and mental health, financial stability, location of the home, community resources, the strength of a social and faith network, self-care, and more.

Similarly, half of people turning 65 will have no private out-of-pocket expenditures for personal care, while more than one in 20 are projected to spend $100,000 or more of their own money. Policy debate that focuses only on income security and acute care—and the corresponding Social Security and Medicare programs—misses the third, largely private risk that retirees face: that of needing long-term care services.

The study confirms that over 72 percent of those needing long term care must use their own funds—that's half of everyone in America. Of those that need care and have to pay for it, the average costs are over $25,000 (2015 dollars) over their lifetime. Other facts made clear, Medicare is projected to only cover 12 percent of the nation's long term care costs, Medicaid is projected to only cover 30 percent of the population, and over 75 percent of people have not discussed care options with their family.

What goes through your head knowing half of the 65 plus group have no private financial resources for personal care expenses? Are you one of them? My parents had a long-term care plan that involved 3 offspring. I do not have that resource. Perhaps neither do you.

Budgeting

Feeling financially secure requires knowing what your assets and liabilities are, and how your income compares to the expenses. If you aren't tracking these, you might not have a complete grasp of the situation. For money security, create a budget that addresses the current needs, like food, clothing and shelter, and the long-term goals, like paying down debt and saving more money. Always include insurance to cover the what-ifs in life.

Do you shop around for better rates for the Internet, cell, cable, car insurance, and other memberships? New customers receive better deals than existing customers. Each year when the contract is up, shop for a new one.

Make a list of the essential expenses: Separate your "wants" from the "needs." Needs include: Monthly rent or mortgage payment, car payment, fuel, public transportation, shared rides, utilities, food, insurance, Internet, cable, and phone bills. Where are you spending needlessly? Spend 50 percent of your take-home pay on needs, 30 percent on wants, and put the remaining 20 percent toward savings and any debts you have. (Here's how I spend my paycheck: 30 percent goes to needs and 20 percent or less goes to wants. At the end of each month, I am able to save 50 percent of the pay. This has helped me save a lot.)

Budget — create a list or spreadsheet and plan how you want to spend money. Following a budget will help you to keep an eye on where it goes. When a person knows where most is spent, then she knows where to pull the reins. Make a plan and the money will not vanish from the bank account. Stay laser focused on getting out of debt and be consistent.

Avoid debt — If you charge something on a credit card, pay it off each month. When you shop, pay with cash or debit cards. Cash gives more spending power. Having no monthly debts will leave more to save.

Few things I did to be debt free: Cancel cable or satellite and watched my favorite shows online. I use a digital antenna and stream movies via Amazon Prime. Eat at home. It's healthier and cheaper to eat what you cook. Invite friends over for a potluck and share a meal instead of meeting at a restaurant. Avoid coffee shops. Stock up on my favorite coffee brands when on sale. Visit the library. This is where I go for books. I haven't bought a book in years. Why should I when the library has them for free? Plus, rent movies for free as well. Cancel the gym membership. Practice yoga and do stretches at home and take long walks for exercise.

Find an accountability partner — encourage a friend to buddy up. Hold one another accountable by creating a budget, then sharing the budget and report back at the end of the month to tally up and compare. The one who fails at staying within the budget has to cook dinner for the other or clean their home.

Long-Term Goals

Pay yourself first—make sure you're setting aside money for long-range goals, like a trip, a move, downsizing the home, or a retirement account. If you're struggling to find enough remaining money to pay down debt, look for discretionary expenses that you can cut. Go free as often as you can. Get books and DVDs from the local library. Take advantage of city parks. Go for long walks and enjoy the local neighborhood, hiking trails, and surroundings. This saves spending money on gym memberships and entertainment. A lot of cities offer free outdoor concerts in the summers or outdoor movies.

My neighbors and I share costs—we buy in bulk and then split the items and share the cost. This saves on buying too much of any one thing. We also attend farmers markets and co-ops to buy bulk fresh foods.

Setting a budget: You can't just set a budget and forget it, you need to verify you're on track and adhere to goals. Ask yourself: What does having enough financial resources last mean to me? Don't hold back. Write everything and anything that comes to mind.

Emergency Fund

Whether you call it an emergency account, a savings account or a rainy day fund, setting aside several months worth of living expenses is critical. That way, when something unexpected comes along like dental work or new tires, refrigerator, or going to the hospital, you have the funds to pay for it rather than going into debt.

I still follow a tight budget. I don't like it but it's reality. I have few complaints because others are worse off. I'm grateful for what I do have; excellent health, a home and vehicle that's paid off, nutritious food, dear friends, a loving extended family, and a safe lifestyle.

Extra Income

My parents retired with three sources of income: savings, pensions, and Social Security. But that's not the case for retirees today. With the decline of pensions and financial markets, older adults have less income to rely one. Bringing in extra money can make a difference when living on a fixed budget. Even if you've already stopped working and getting Social Security, a part- or full-time job can help offset expenses.

A member of the Elder Orphan Group, Joyce Teal, a former teacher has reinvented herself as an art and fitness instructor. Her creative career has included commissioned quilting, published pattern designer, and participated in juried art shows for over 30 years. Joyce enjoys extra income from a home based business but not the kind like Avon, driving for Uber, or selling someone else's product or service. Instead, it's a product, skill, or service that she uniquely provides to a select customer base. See her advice below.

Are you ready to start a home business?

- Are you ready for the challenges of a home-based business? Do you have a place to run one? You'll need a computer, printer FAX, internet, telephone, a small filing cabinet for papers, records, customer orders, and possibly mailing supplies, and materials. The dining room table might seem like a good place to work and the china cabinet as storage but if you have to move work away for eating. Choose a space where you can "close the door" at the end of the day.

- Do you have a service or skill that people will pay for? Learn the competition through research: What do they deliver? What do they charge? Can you personalize the service or add value? Are you charging enough to cover expenses and earn a fair wage? If you don't make a profit and pay yourself a fair wage, it's not a business. The IRS will call it a hobby and you lose valuable deductions on your taxes.

- Do you have a product that people will buy? Do you have to invest in products to sell? Amazon, Cafe Press, and eBay have wholesale departments to buy products in bulk to resell and they will ship products and handle payment collection for a small fee. They will send you a check every month based on sales.

- If you carry inventory at home, do you have storage space and a place to prepare items for shipping? We live in an "instant" world and people want their orders tomorrow so easy and fast access to a mailing source is priority.

- If you have a service to offer, do you need to upgrade your technology? Do you have reliable transportation? How will you collect payments? PayPal, Vemo, Google Wallet, and Apple Pay are good choices to receive payments. Check with your bank regarding ways to receive money into your separate business account.

- Do you have a service to offer? Often doing blogs, vlogs, and YouTube videos will allow you to become an affiliate with companies that offer services and products that complement your business. Additionally, you can sell advertising on your online presence to other companies that target your followers.

- What are the legal and tax regulations? This varies state to state, county to county, even locally. Do you need a resale license? Do you have to collect sales tax? Do you need to be bonded? What licenses do your city, county, or state require? Check with your insurance company for coverage for your car, anything you purchased to run your business, and inventory. Usually, a simple rider will cover a business and inventory. If you are a renter or have an HOA, will they require a permit? Check IRS.gov to learn about tax-related obligations.

- Can you manage time? Are you organized? Can you manage the technology needed for your business? You must separate the business from your personal life. This is a great challenge as a home-based business owner. People expect businesses to be available 24/7 and will quickly move to another business if you aren't available.

- The sky's the limit! Take a look at your hobbies and what interests you. Chances are you are not alone and there are others with similar interests. Does this seem overwhelming? Yes, it is daunting! Go back to the beginning of this exercise and start answering the questions on paper or the computer. It will be enlightening!

As for me, I work and will continue to work part-time for as long as I'm able and enjoy it. A job will keep me active, mentally challenged, and connected with people. That's thriving!

SMART LEGAL MATTERS

Every adult needs a Will, a Health care power of attorney, a Durable power of attorney, a Living will, and a Revocable trust. Each one signed, dated, notarized as necessary and kept in a safe place that someone else knows about and can retrieve on a moment's notice. In these, you name a trusted person to make healthcare and financial decisions on your behalf, if you are no longer able. This doesn't have to be the same person, but it can be. In older age, a person needs a trusted legal guardian or proxy to uphold their wishes. It's best to work with an estate planning attorney to arrange the proper legal documents.

These documents have names that sound alike, so make sure to get the ones that fit your circumstances. State laws vary, so learn about the rules, requirements, and forms used in your State.

Wills and trusts let you name the person you want your money and property to go to after you die.

Advance directives (aka, health care power of attorney) lets you make arrangements for care if sick. Two common types of advance directives are:

- A living will gives you a say in your health care if you become too sick to make your wishes known. In a living will, you can state what kind of care you do or don't want. This can make it easier for family members to make tough healthcare decisions for you.

- A durable power of attorney for health care lets you name the person you want to make medical decisions for you if you can't make them yourself. Make sure the person you name is willing to make those decisions for you.

For legal matters, there are ways to give someone you trust the power to act in your place.

- A general power of attorney lets you give someone else the authority to act on your behalf, but this power will end if you are unable to make your own decisions.

- A durable power of attorney allows you to name someone to act on your behalf for any legal task, but it stays in place if you become unable to make your own decisions.

Living will is a legal document that spells out medical treatments you would and would not want to be used to keep you alive, as well as your preferences for other medical decisions, such as pain management or organ donation. In determining preferences and wishes, consider your values. Ask yourself: How important it is to me to be independent and self-sufficient? In what circumstances would I feel like it's not worth living? Would I want treatment to extend life in any situation? All situations? Do I want treatment only if a cure is possible?

When considering the medical treatments—talk with your doctor.

List of treatments to review

- Cardiopulmonary resuscitation (CPR) restarts the heart when it has stopped beating. Ask yourself: Under what circumstances would I want to be resuscitated by CPR or by a device that delivers a therapeutic shock?

- Mechanical ventilation takes over your breathing if you're unable to breathe on your own. Ask yourself: How long would I want to be placed on a mechanical ventilator?

- Tube feeding supplies the body with nutrients and fluids intravenously or via a tube in the stomach. Ask yourself: How long would I want to be fed by this device?

- Dialysis removes waste from your blood and manages fluid levels if your kidneys no longer function. Ask yourself: When and for how long would I want to receive this treatment?

- Antibiotics or antiviral medications can be used to treat many infections. Ask yourself: If near the end of life, would I want infections to be treated aggressively or let them run their course?

- Comfort care (palliative care) are interventions to keep you comfortable and manage pain while abiding by your treatment wishes. Ask yourself: If I choose to die at home, what types of palliative procedures do I want to receive? Pain medications? Fed ice chips to soothe mouth dryness? To avoid invasive tests or treatments?

- Organ and tissue donations for transplantation should be specified. If your organs are removed for donation, you will be kept on life-sustaining treatments temporarily until complete. Help your health care agent avoid confusion by stating in the living will that you understand the need for this temporary intervention.

- Donating your body for scientific study. Contact a local medical school, university or donation program for information on how to register for a planned donation.

Revocable trust is a legal document that places the grantor's assets into a trust during their lifetime and then distributes to heirs or beneficiaries after death. The grantor (you) can change or cancel the trust while alive. Typically, a revocable trust is used to avoid probate court.

Interview with Kerry R. Peck, Managing Partner, PECK RITCHEY LLC (Chicago)

To help adults best prepare in the legal affairs, I asked a long-time colleague, Kerry R. Peck, past president of the Chicago Bar Association, several questions. Peck is a vigilant advocate for adults and families that may be victims of financial exploitation. Mr. Peck co-authored the book, Alzheimer's and the Law, published by the American Bar Association. He is the recipient of the 2014 Justice John Paul Stevens Award, the Chicago Bar Association's highest honor. He was also selected by IIT Chicago-Kent College of Law as one of their 125 Alumni of Distinction.

When drawing up the legal docs and selecting a Power of Attorney, Health care Proxy and other legal matters, what advice do you have for adults living alone?

Kerry R. Peck: The selection of an agent for your Power of Attorney (POA) or as a health care proxy should be based on trust and the nature of the friendship/relationship between you and the potential agent/proxy. Age should not be a deciding factor, while at the same time, you certainly do not want to pick someone considerably older than you. You should pick an agent/proxy who is willing to implement your wishes particularly in end-of-life decision making. You should choose an agent/proxy who loves you a lot more than they love your money.

How often should a client review the legal decisions? Every 5 years?

Kerry R. Peck: As the life circumstances change, review the documents. Follow the guideline: Did you get divorced? Did the recipient of your bequest of money under your will or your agent under POA die? Did you have a new child or new grandchild? Major life changes require review of your estate planning documents. Certainly, every five years would be the maximum for potential review of the documents or if there's any major changes of the law.

For those with little or no family, what do you recommend they do?

Kerry R. Peck: Your support network of friends, place of worship members, senior center and other professionals should provide ample choices for the selection of a trustee named in your revocable living trust, an executor named in your will and agent named in your POA or proxy named in your health care POA. In addition, banks can act as trustee, executor and sometimes POA for property.

Under what circumstances do you recommend selecting this professional to stand for me, a person living alone?

Kerry R. Peck: Many attorneys and law firms will act as fiduciaries. They will act as a trustee in a revocable living trust, executor named in a will and agent under POA for property. You probably would not name your attorney as your agent for health care unless you have been friends with the lawyer for many years and they are aware of your wishes, desires and end of life decision making.

What about legal guardians? Under what circumstances do you recommend selecting this professional to stand for a person aging alone? (I hear horror stories.. even patient advocates— friends of mine—do not recommend them.)

Kerry R. Peck: The appointment of a legal guardian is required only when no advanced planning is done. Guardianship is avoidable through use of: Revocable Living Trust, POA for Property, and POA for Health Care. Most attorneys would rather be the counsel for the guardian, rather than be the guardian.

Guardianship is a court-supervised proceeding in which the court must approve expenditures, location of residence, investments pursuant to statute and should be used only in appropriate circumstances. Often guardianships are contested proceedings because the alleged disabled person who is the subject of the guardianship does not believe they need help in the management of their affairs or health care decision making. Guardianship is a determination whether a person needs a 3rd party decision maker to be made related to asset management and health care decisions.

Any pitfalls to look for?

Kerry R. Peck: Don't be a victim of undue influence by a friend, caregiver or someone who is interested in your assets. Use your intuition. Choose your friends wisely. Someone who is new to your life and wants to be your best friend is not always someone you should trust.

As reflected in the interview with Kerry R. Peck, estate planning is the process of legally structuring current and projected assets for future allocation and disposal. An estate plan eliminates the uncertainties over probate administration of assets and maximizes the value of a families' or individual's estate by reducing taxes and other expenses.

And because half of the people over 65 who are admitted to a hospital — are unable to make decisions for themselves[5], a healthcare proxy is urgent.

There are many online resources to help you consider and create your wishes and learn how to discuss them with family, friends, and medical providers. I've discovered that the standard advance directive forms that people can download aren't enough to safeguard one's wishes, nor do they ensure your wishes are followed in the event you can not speak for yourself. What's needed: Document the well thought out decisions that reflect your wishes and values, and to have deep and personal conversations with your medical decision-makers before a crisis occurs.

Health Care Proxy

There are several key points in choosing an ideal healthcare proxy. Begin by talking about your wishes and finding out if the person will follow them. As stated by Kerry R. Peck, choose a person <u>you trust</u> with your life and you know they will follow your wishes ahead of their own. It's best if the person takes a careful and calm approach to solving problems. Someone who ranks high with critical thinking skills:

- A healthcare proxy requires the ability to absorb information and ask clarifying questions.

- Make sure you clearly articulate and communicate your wishes, your medical conditions, and what procedures you want or do not want.

These questions will help you assess and choose the best healthcare proxy.

- Will this person speak for you in case you cannot?

- Act on your wishes and separate their own feelings from yours?

- Live close by or could travel to be with you?

- Knows you well and understands what you want?

- Is someone you trust with your life?

- Will talk with you about sensitive issues?

- Will it be available long-term?

- Able to handle conflicting opinions between family, friends and medical team?

- Is a strong advocate in the face of an unresponsive doctor or institution?

What to Consider in a Health Care Proxy?

Selecting the ideal agent is an important decision, and likely one of the toughest you will make in planning. The person you select will make healthcare decisions on your behalf in time(s) you are not able to for yourself. As stated before, choose someone you trust with your life and you know s/he will follow your wishes ahead of his/her feelings or beliefs. It's best if the person selected take a careful and calm approach to solving problems. Someone who ranks high with critical thinking skills.

Top Five Critical Thinking Skills

- Analytical. Have the ability to carefully examine something, whether it is a problem, a set of data, or a text.

- Communication. How clearly does the person share their conclusions with you or a group of decision makers?

- Creativity. Can they think outside the box and come up with ideas or solutions no one has considered?

- Open-Minded. Can they put aside assumptions or judgments and analyze the information they receive?

- Are they direct when asking questions? Or do they beat around the bush?

- Problem Solving. Can they come up with practical solutions?

A health care proxy requires the ability to absorb information and ask clarifying questions. Make sure you clearly articulate and communicate your wishes, your medical conditions, what procedures you want administered or not.

Other factors:

- Location. The selected proxy does not need to live with you, under the same roof, or even in the same town, but don't select someone far away in case decisions require immediate attention.

- Name a secondary health care proxy as backup.

- Most people select family members to be the proxy, but you can consider a friend instead. Your doctor cannot be your healthcare proxy. If you have siblings or more than one child, think which one meets these personal characteristics, regardless of birth order, age, or profession.

Checklist to Assess, Clarify, and Communicate Medical Needs

Exercise: This particular checklist does not create a formal advance directive but it is the one my attorney gave me to assess, clarify, and communicate what is important in the event of a serious illness.

When is the right time to choose a proxy? When you reach 18 years of age because your parents are no longer the automatic proxy. When getting married or divorced. Reevaluate when life circumstances change. NOW, if you don't have one. When diagnosed with a serious disease or condition. Upon the death of a spouse.

Assess and choose the best healthcare proxy

Will this person speak for me in case I am unable? Act on my wishes and separate their own feelings from mine? Live close by or could travel to be with me? Knows me well (I know well) and understands what I want? Is a person I trust with my life? Will you talk with me about sensitive issues? Will the person be available long-term? Able to handle conflicting opinions between family, friends, and medical team? Can I be a strong advocate in the face of an unresponsive doctor or institution?

When arranging your Advanced Health Directives, ask yourself: What medical treatments and care are acceptable to me? Are there some that I would absolutely not choose? Do I wish to be resuscitated (revived) if I stop breathing and the heart stops? You need a DNR (Do Not Resuscitate) to specify your choice to continue or not.

Duties and Tasks of a Health Care Proxy

Share these duties with the person(s) you will interview for the position. The proxy is in charge of making health care decisions on behalf of the person they're representing in the event s/he is not able to make decisions. The proxy/agent will be the eyes, ears, and speech for that person. Serving in this role, the proxy will also observe in the specific way s/he wants health care decisions carried out. And as they agent, you will be responsible for making sure her/his wishes are honored.

The decisions a proxy will make

- Choices about medical care, medical tests and procedures, medicine, and/or surgery

- The right to request or decline life-support treatments

- Pain management choices, and authorizing or refusing specific medication or procedures or treatments

- Where the person will receive medical treatment, including the right to move the person to another facility, hospital, or state, or to a nursing home or hospice facility

- The option to take legal action on the person's behalf in order to advocate for his/her health care rights and wishes

- Apply for Medicare, Medicaid, or other programs or insurance benefits on the person's behalf

- Learn about the medical condition and treatment options

- Communicate with the medical team, and ask questions about the condition, treatments, and options

- Review the medical chart

- Communicate with the family about the condition and treatment plan

- Access and approve release of the medical records

- Request and coordinate second opinions or outside care

Once you have signed and witnessed the advance care directive, make sure your doctors, health care proxy, family members, clergy, and any others you want involved in your care have copies.

Medical Decisions

Everyone will have to make healthcare decisions at some point in their lives, either for themselves, their family members, or both. Consider the following four principles:

- The pros and cons of each option

- The risks of each option

- The cost of each option

- Your personal preferences

When your healthcare provider suggests surgery, a new medication, a medical test or any other type of care, ask why. What are the treatment goals and what will happen if I choose not to follow the advice? Are there other options? What are the risks involved with the procedure or the side effects? Do the risks outweigh the benefits? How likely is it that this treatment will address the problem? What does each option cost?

The goal is to understand what the recommendation entails in order to make an informed decision. What to understand: medicines come with side effects, medical tests can give false results, and surgery comes with risks. When faced with health decisions, your goals and values are just as important as the medical facts. Ask yourself: What matters to me most? What is my desired outcome?

Faith Decisions

Ask yourself: What are your fears regarding the end of life? Do you want to be sedated if it were necessary to control pain? Does it matter if the drugs make you drowsy or puts you to sleep most of the time? Do you want a hospice team or palliative care available? Are there people to whom you want to write a letter or prepare a recorded message — to open later by them? How do you want to be remembered?

What are your wishes for a memorial service? How would you describe your faith? What do you want others to know about your beliefs? What gives your life purpose and meaning? What do you need for comfort at the end? What priorities do you want others to know?

Find a trustworthy person or family you can depend on for support and care. Work out a payment strategy and put it in writing. Get legal advice before implementing a plan. An elder law attorney can steer you in the right direction.

Steps for Getting Your Affairs in Order

- Put your important papers and copies of legal documents in one place. You can set up a file, put everything in a desk or dresser drawer, or list the information and location of papers in a notebook. If your papers are in a bank safe deposit box, keep copies in a file at home. Check each year to see if there's anything new to add.

- Tell a trusted family member or friend where you put all your important papers. You don't need to tell this friend or family member about your personal affairs, but someone should know where you keep your papers in case of an emergency. If you don't have a relative or friend you trust, ask a lawyer to help.

- Discuss your end-of-life preferences with your doctor. He or she can explain what <u>health decisions you may have to make</u> in the future and what treatment options are available. <u>Talking with your doctor</u> can help ensure your wishes are honored. Discussing advance care planning decisions with your doctor is free through Medicare during your annual wellness visit. Private health insurance may also cover these discussions.

- Give permission in advance for your doctor or lawyer to talk with your caregiver as needed. There may be questions about your care, a bill, or a health insurance claim. Without your consent, your caregiver may not be able to get needed information. You can give your okay in advance to Medicare, a credit card company, your bank, or your doctor. You may need to sign and return a form. (Source: National Institute of Health)

SMART FUN | ENGAGEMENT

Smiling looks good, feels good, and is contagious. It increases endorphins and other mood-enhancing hormones. Smiling calms the heart rate and blood pressure, reduces stress, heightens a sense of well-being, and supports good health. Dale Carnegie believed in his popular 1936 book, How to Win Friends & Influence People, that the act of smiling will make people like you. Carnegie quoted a Chinese proverb: "a man without a smiling face must not open a shop." Your smile is a messenger of goodwill, and an easy way to make a good impression. Carnegie advised readers to smile even when they don't feel like it, because action and feeling go together. When a person smiles, they feel happier, and that could influence others around them.

Laugh

Mayo Clinic tells us that a good laugh has great short-term effects. When you laugh, it doesn't just lighten your load mentally, it actually induces physical changes in the body. Laughter can:

- Stimulates organs. Laughter enhances your intake of oxygen, stimulates the heart, lungs and muscles, and increases the endorphins.

- Relieves stress response. A rollicking laugh fires up and then cools down your stress response, and it can increase and then decrease your heart rate and blood pressure. The result? A good, relaxed feeling.

- Soothe tension. Laughter stimulates circulation and aids muscle relaxation, both of which reduce the physical symptoms of stress.

The long-term benefits:

- Improves the immune system. Negative thoughts manifest into chemical reactions that can affect the body and create stress and decrease immunity. By contrast, positive thoughts can actually release neuropeptides that help fight stress and potentially serious illnesses.

- Relieve pain. Laughter may ease pain by causing the body to produce its own natural painkillers.

- Increase personal satisfaction. Laughter can also make it easier to cope with difficult situations. It also helps you connect with other people.

- Improves mood. Many people experience depression, sometimes due to chronic illnesses. Laughter can help lessen stress, depression and anxiety. It can also improve self-esteem.

Developing a sense of humor[6] may be easier than one thinks. Is your sense of humor underdeveloped — or nonexistent?No worries. It can be learned.

- Start the day by reading funny comics in the newspaper or watch a quick video on YouTube that strikes a smile.

- Find photos or greeting cards that are funny. Then hang them up at home or collect them in your journal. Watch funny movies and comedy videos. Look online at joke websites or silly videos.

- Listen to humorous podcasts. Go to a comedy club. Take an Impromptu acting class.

- Spend time with friends who make you laugh.

- Browse through a bookstore or library's joke books and add a few jokes to your list.

- Try laughter yoga. In laughter yoga, people practice laughter as a group. Laughter is forced at first, but it can soon turn into spontaneous laughter.

Add Positive Experiences

Add variety to your morning routine. Do you usually eat breakfast at the table? Take your breakfast out to the porch and listen to the birds sing. Do you typically start the day by working out at the gym? Take physical activity outdoors by walking on a nature trail. While on the walk, observe infants and young children delight and amuse in the most ordinary things.

Challenge your values

What do you want to be remembered for? Answer that question and challenge yourself to make it happen.

- Dance. Crank up your favorite 60's, 70's, 80's, or 90's jam and dance at home. You might feel silly, but I dare you to try this and tell me it wasn't fun.

- Entertain. Ask yourself, "If I had a close friend coming into town to visit and had 24 hours to make sure they had a heck of a time, where would I take them?" Make a plan to answer that question and then go do all of those things yourself—or invite someone along.

- Go outside and listen to the crickets chirping, birds singing and wind blowing. Focus really hard and be amazed by the beautiful nature sounds that you've been too busy to notice.

- What subject matter fascinates you? Read an article per day about it. If repeated over weeks and months, you'll be so well-versed. Then a Facebook page or blog for the purpose of educating others. The material gives a batch of conversation starters, no matter the outing.

- Take up a yoga or spin class. Feel artsy? Learn a new craft like stitching, pottery, or painting. If you'd like to increase your confidence and public speaking, join an acting class or audition for a community theater. If you want to learn how to protect yourself, find a self-defense or martial-arts class.

- Volunteer at animal shelters, children's museums, and soup kitchens. Choose an activity that grabs your heart and fill time by making the world a better place.

- Go people watching—my neighbor and I visit a nearby mall occasionally just to watch the shoppers. We buy a cup of coffee and sit on a bench. And then watch the bustling shoppers and make up stories about their lives.

- Avoid negativity—conversations, news, entertainment, etc., that frightens, upsets or

- distresses you, or makes you feel sad and unhappy.

- Be responsive to a friend. Ask a question you've been putting off, because you thought you didn't have time to talk about it.

- Strike Up a Conversation with a stranger. It might feel intimidating at first but it is so fulfilling. Strike up a chat with the woman serving you coffee, the family in front of you at the grocery store, or a new co-worker who seems a little shy.

CHAPTER 6.
SMART RESOURCES

You're ready to remedy the challenges and to find solutions. Here are the websites, blogs, YouTube videos that I use. However, consider your own favorite news sources, articles, blogs, and websites to gather information and data. Google or other search engine keyword searches are a smart way to increase knowledge and information, especially when doing local searches. Be sure to use the factors of an issue in the search term, plus city, county and state. And then save the results in a document. The more you know— the faster you'll discover viable options for a better future.

SMART HEALTH | FITNESS RESOURCES

Knowing is Not Enough—Act on Your Family Health History

What are your risks of certain diseases?

With a doctor, determine if you need a specific genetic test. Is there a condition you're not aware of? Has your healthcare team procured all preventative medical tests including blood?

How to Collect Your Family Health History https://www.cdc.gov/genomics/famhistory/knowing_not_enough.htm

My Family Health Portrait http://kahuna.clayton.edu/jqu/FHH/html/index.html

Recording Your Family Medical Resources https://www.verywellhealth.com/recording-family-medical-history-2615513

Annual blood test results and screenings

A good resource for understanding blood tests: what they show and more. https://www.healthline.com/health/blood-tests#top-blood-tests

Diet and Nutrition

USDA Dietary Guidelines and Harvard's Healthy Eating Plate: https://health.gov/our-work/nutrition-physical-activity/dietary-guidelines/previous-dietary-guidelines/2015

Harvard's Healthy Eating Plate: https://www.hsph.harvard.edu/nutritionsource/healthy-eating-plate/.

Diet and Nutrition Resources

Centers for Disease Control http://www.cdc.gov/

Environmental Protection Agency http://www.epa.gov

Environmental Working Group Consumer Guides http://www.ewg.org/consumer-guides

Harvard's Healthy Eating Plate http://www.health.harvard.edu/plate/healthy-eating-plate

National Eating Disorders Association http://www.nationaleatingdisorders.org/

Turn the Tide Foundation http://www.turnthetidefoundation.org/

USDA Center for Nutrition Policy and Promotion http://www.cnpp.usda.gov/

USDHHS 2015-2020 Dietary Guidelines https://health.gov/dietaryguidelines/2015/

World Health Organization http://www.who.int

Diet and USDA Assessment tools

Dietary Guidance: https://www.nal.usda.gov/legacy/fnic/dietary-guidance-0

Fat intake: https://www.nutritionquest.com/wellness/free-assessment-tools-for-individuals/fat-intake-screener/

Fruit, vegetable, and fiber screening: https://www.nutritionquest.com/wellness/free-assessment-tools-for-individuals/fruit-vegetable-fiber-screener/

Healthy body calculator http://www.dietitian.com/healthy-body-calculator/

Nutrition and whole foods:

Eat Right https://www.eatright.org/food/nutrition/dietary-guidelines-and-myplate/healthy-eating-for-older-adults

Mayo Clinic https://www.mayoclinic.org/healthy-lifestyle/caregivers/in-depth/senior-health/art-20044699

Nutrition.gov https://www.nutrition.gov/topics/nutrition-age/older-individuals

Determine your Nutritional Health at DHS.gov.vi http://www.dhs.gov.vi/home/documents/DetermineNutritionChecklist.pdf

My Self Care Resources

Therapistaid Worksheets https://www.therapistaid.com/worksheets/self-care-assessment.pdf

Developing a Self-care plan http://socialwork.buffalo.edu/resources/self-care-starter-kit/developing-your-self-care-plan.html

Self-care exercises http://socialwork.buffalo.edu/resources/self-care-starter-kit/self-care-assessments-exercises/exercises-and-activities.html

How to Practice Self-care https://positivepsychology.com/self-care-worksheets/

Practice Mindfulness https://www.moniquetallon.com/10-simple-ways-to-practice-mindfulness-in-our-daily-life/

How do I bring more mindfulness into my life https://www.mindful.org/how-do-i-bring-more-mindfulness-into-my-life/

What Is Mindfulness? Psychology Today https://www.psychologytoday.com/blog/click-here-happiness/201902/what-is-mindfulness-and-how-be-more-mindful

Tips for clarifying needs

How to Stop Being a People-Pleaser https://greatergood.berkeley.edu/article/item/how_to_stop_being_a_people_pleaser

Interpersonal Effectiveness https://www.dbtselfhelp.com/html/interpersonal_effectiveness_ha.html

Ways to live from the heart https://gailbrenner.com/2011/10/10-love-filled-ways-to-live-from-your-heart/

Find Purpose | Solo and Smart YouTube https://youtu.be/q5iRD2j2VMo

How to forgive yourself https://www.healthline.com/health/how-to-forgive-yourself

How to Forgive Yourself and Move on From the Past https://www.psychologytoday.com/us/blog/focus-forgiveness/201410/how-forgive-yourself-and-move-the-past

Self Knowledge | Solo and Smart YouTube https://www.youtube.com/playlist?list=PLGHmSaERTYGeBXPKHtd0zxHNRuOYoJNAt

Appreciate Yourself | Solo and Smart YouTube https://youtu.be/S2zp1JHzjc0

How to Appreciate the Person You Are | Solo and Smart YouTube https://youtu.be/YA9DEIEOM5s

Weight Resources

Cost-Effectiveness of Chronic Disease and Healthy Weight Tips for Older Adults.

Cost-Effectiveness of Chronic Disease Interventions https://www.cdc.gov/chronicdisease/programs-impact/pop/index.htm

Healthy Weight Tips for Older Adults https://www.niddk.nih.gov/health-information/weight-management/healthy-eating-physical-activity-for-life/health-tips-for-older-adults

Weight Control https://medlineplus.gov/weightcontrol.html

Fitness Resources

The study on fitness: Journal Neurology https://n.neurology.org/content/86/14/1313

Set Fitness Goals

Set realistic goals and developing an exercise plan. For information on how to set exercise goals and a plan: https://www.nia.nih.gov/health/how-older-adults-can-get-started-exercise#goals. Create and follow the plan. Find an accountability partner to maintain consistency and follow through. Together, come up with an exercise strategy, make it specific, including type, frequency, intensity, and time. Check progress and re-evaluate goals.

Physical activity Tracking tools https://www.nia.nih.gov/health/exercise-and-physical-activity-tracking-tools

Check your local community resources, such as mall-walking groups and senior center fitness classes. To find local groups go to Meetup.com, create a neighborhood group on Nextdoor.com, or check with the local senior centers and the public library for groups nearby.

Preventing Alzheimer's Disease https://consumer.healthday.com/encyclopedia/aging-1/misc-aging-news-10/preventing-alzheimer-s-648930.html

Fitness Peer Support https://www.heart.org/en/healthy-living/fitness/staying-motivated/dont-work-out-alone—fitness-peer-support

Online Support Group Could Help You Meet Your Goals https://www.shape.com/weight-loss/tips-plans/online-support-group-could-help-you-meet-goals

Facebook Groups for Fitness and Motivation https://www.verywellfit.com/facebook-groups-for-fitness-and-motivation-4150657d

Emotional Health Resources
Emotional Wellness Toolkit https://www.nih.gov/health-information/emotional-wellness-toolkit
How to Identify Your Strengths and Weaknesses https://www.wikihow.com/Identify-Your-Strengths-and-Weaknesses
Self-knowledge Solo and Smart YouTube
Inspiring Resolutions to Make You a Better Human https://youtu.be/3SrlcbzKaQ0
Intention with Purpose https://youtu.be/q5iRD2j2VMo
Manage Stress Solo and Smart YouTube https://www.youtube.com/playlist?list=PLGHmSaERTYGcNhj6YvvFt_JWESCKG1gsU
Emotional Health for Older Adults YouTube https://www.youtube.com/results?search_query=emotional+health+for+seniors

Mobility Resources
Plan to Stay Safe, Mobile, and Independent https://www.cdc.gov/injury/features/older-adults-mobility/index.html
Walking https://www.health.harvard.edu/blog/walking-exercise-helps-seniors-stay-mobile-independent-201405287173
How to Improve Mobility https://www.salmonhealth.com/blog/how-to-increase-mobility-in-older-adults/
Stretching Exercises for Seniors to Improve Mobility https://www.healthline.com/health/senior-health/stretching-exercises#5
Stretching Exercises to Improve Mobility YouTube https://www.youtube.com/results?search_query=Stretching+Exercises+for+Seniors+to+Improve+Mobility

Chronic Diseases and Managing Them Resources
Chronic Disease Cost Study https://www.cdc.gov/chronicdisease/about/index.htm

The National Council on Aging distributes proven programs in-person and online that empower individuals to manage their own care and improve their quality of life. https://www.ncoa.org/healthy-aging/chronic-disease/

Chronic Disease Self-Management Education https://www.ncoa.org/healthy-aging/chronic-disease/chronic-disease-self-management-programs/

Fall Risk and Fracture risk—results of a DEXA scan How well do you practice fall prevention and balance and strength exercises?

Fracture Risk Resources

Learn about FRAX score and treatment https://www.medicalnewstoday.com/articles/frax-score#treatment

Falls Prevention https://www.ncoa.org/healthy-aging/falls-prevention/

Why Older People Fall & How to Reduce Fall Risk https://betterhealthwhileaging.net/why-aging-adults-fall/

Falls prevention exercises for seniors YouTube https://www.youtube.com/results?search_query=fall+prevention+exercises+for+seniors

11 Balance Exercises for Seniors https://www.healthline.com/health/exercise-fitness/balance-exercises-for-seniors

Balance Exercises YouTube Balance exercises for older adults

Mood Resources

APA Stress Tips https://www.apa.org/topics/stress/tips

Good Therapy—learn about mood swings https://www.goodtherapy.org/learn-about-therapy/issues/mood-swings

Sleep Resources

National Sleep Foundation https://www.thensf.org

Medical News Today https://www.medicalnewstoday.com/articles/325353

Forks Over Knives Wellness https://www.forksoverknives.com/wellness/healthy-sleep-hygiene-habits-101/

Find a Good Doctor Resources

Discussing Health Decisions with Your Doctor https://www.nia.nih.gov/health/discussing-health-decisions-your-doctor

Tools to help you choose doctors, hospitals, and health care facilities https://www.usa.gov/doctors

Find the right doctor with these online resources https://www.cnet.com/how-to/find-the-right-doctor-with-these-online-resources/

Choosing a good primary care doctor https://www.consumerreports.org/doctors/how-to-find-a-good-doctor/

What Should I Ask My Doctor During a Checkup? https://www.nia.nih.gov/health/what-should-i-ask-my-doctor-during-checkup

Improved Functional Ability Resources

How to increase the number of steps https://thehealthsessions.com/walking-10000-steps-a-day/

Improve posture https://thehealthsessions.com/the-simplest-posture-exercise/

Exercises for chronic illnesses https://thehealthsessions.com/exercises-for-chronic-health-conditions/

Expert Advice: Overcome obstacles to exercising with chronic illness https://thehealthsessions.com/exercising-with-chronic-illness/

How to Decrease Fall Risk and Improve Functional Mobility https://www.medbridgeeducation.com/blog/2017/08/decrease-fall-risk-improve-functional-mobility/

SMART HOUSING | LOCATION RESOURCES
Modifying Your Home

Age in Place Self-Assessment

Receive a professional assessment of your quality of life from a geriatric care manager or care coordinator. In this checklist, a number of elements are assessed. http://agis.com/Document/30/what-a-professional-assessment-covers-checklist.html

Find and locate care managers, architects, and contractors for home modifications.

Care Manager — Aging Life Care management, is a holistic, client-centered approach to caring for older adults or others facing ongoing health challenges. https://www.aginglifecare.org/ALCAWEB/What_is_Aging_Life_Care/Search/Find_an_Expert.aspx

Architect Directory https://architects.regionaldirectory.us/

National Aging in Place Council - a senior support network that connects service providers with older homeowners, their families, and caretakers. https://ageinplace.org/

Certified Senior Advisor — educates and certifies professionals who work with seniors through its Working with Older Adults education program and the Certified Senior Advisor credential. https://www.csa.us/

National Association of Home Builders - Remodel Your Home https://www.nahb.org/search#q=directory&t=coveo79b6ec88&sort=relevancy

Home Advisors — find trusted local pros for any home project. https://www.homeadvisor.com/

TaskRabbit— allows you to have approved help at your home the same day for a variety of small jobs and chores. https://www.taskrabbit.com/

Dwell — trained architects are able to help people take their project to the next level. https://www.dwell.com/best/architects

Houzz — Get inspired. Shop products. Find pros. https://www.houzz.com/

Review lab — home improvement resource guide. http://www.reviewlab.com/home-improvement-guide/

Thumbtack — find a handyman near you. https://www.thumbtack.com/k/handyman/

Association of Certified Handyman Professionals https://handymanassociation.org/

Home modifications and products to help you get around. Use this list to identify accessibility, safety and security issues and fall hazards. http://agis.com/Document/13/home-safety-and-security-checklist.html

Additional housing ideas

Eldercare Locator: Housing options for older adults https://www.n4a.org/files/HousingOptions.pdf

Resources to help you find the right place and the right house https://www.marketwatch.com/story/should-you-move-in-your-50s-or-60s-how-to-choose-where-to-live-in-retirement-11634917932

Right Place, Right Time Assessment https://www.smartliving360.com/

Life Plan Community — ask if they provide at home care services —if you want to stay home but have few to rely on for help, check out this guide for services that are available through senior housing communities. Also, contact the local assisted living, or independent living communities for services they may offer to you at home. https://www.humangood.org/life-plan-community-complete-guide

Alzheimer's Association — Call the local office for at home care services — organizations catering to older adults offer outstanding research and resources for locals https://www.alz.org/
Jewish Family Services - contact the local agency for available home services.
Faith Organizations - contact your local church, synagogue, mosque, and other places of worship for available home services and help.
Meals on Wheels of America helps people avoid hunger https://www.mealsonwheelsamerica.org/
Find Assisted Living—Nationwide directory of over 36,000 facilities https://www.seniorcare.com/assisted-living/
Find Skilled Nursing—Nationwide directory of over 15,000 facilities https://www.seniorcare.com/nursing-homes/
Find Home Care—Nationwide directory of over 37,000 facilities https://www.seniorcare.com/home-care/
Find Adult Day Care—Nationwide directory of over 4,000 facilities https://www.seniorcare.com/adult-day-care/
National Shared Housing Resource https://nationalsharedhousing.org/
Silvernest Find a Housemate - Find a Roommate https://www.silvernest.com/
Roommates.com https://www.roommates.com
Roomster.com Rooms for rents https://www.roomster.com/
Village to Village Network—Neighbors Caring for Neighbors! Villages are community-based, nonprofit, grassroots organizations formed through neighbors who want to change the paradigm of aging. https://www.vtvnetwork.org/
Naturally Occurring Retirement Community https://www.giaging.org/initiatives/age-friendly/age-friendly-resources/choosing-an-approach/naturally-occurring-retirement-communities-norc

VOA Helps Seniors, Families, Vets & People With Special Needs Find Homes. https://www.voa.org

AARP — Livability Index https://www.aarp.org/ppi/issues/livable-communities/info-2015/livability-index.html and https://videos.aarp.org/detail/video/5822037804001/part-ii:-livability-index-relaunch---aarp

American Planning Association —Creating Great Communities for all https://planning.org/blog/9228233/design-thinking-new-approach-to-solving-planning-challenges/

Shared Housing Resources

Location Resources

Livability https://livability.com/methodology-ranking-criteria/

Where is the best place for me to live? LANA, the App https://www.bestplaces.net/fybp/

Explore where to move based on your personal preferences—Teleport https://teleport.org

Find your best place to live https://www.maptitan.com

Walkscore https://www.walkscore.com

HUD Rental Assistance https://www.hud.gov/topics/rental_assistance

Village to Village Network - learn about the village movement helping people age in place https://www.vtvnetwork.org

Helpful Village - helping older adults age in place https://www.helpfulvillage.com/what-is-a-village

PropertyShark.com https://www.propertyshark.com/Real-Estate-Reports/20-us-cities-mild-climate-affordable-housing)

Worldwide Weather and Climate information https://weather-and-climate.com

Need for care checklists http://agis.com/eldercare-checklist/

Support Services http://agis.com/Eldercare-Basics/Support-Services/index-2.html

Age in Place Guide https://www.retireguide.com/guides/aging-in-place/

Proximity to Friends
The Framingham Heart Study https://framinghamheartstudy.org
Benefits of Nearby Friends
The Nurses' Health Study from Harvard Medical School, Benefits of
Nearby Friends https://nurseshealthstudy.org

SMART SOCIAL CONNECTION RESOURCES
Daily social interactions
6 Strategies for Improving Emotional Health https://www.nih.gov/
health-information/emotional-wellness-toolkit
Questions to ask your best friends https://www.persuadeed.com/100-
best-questions-to-ask-your-friends-about-yourself/
Develop True Intimacy https://newayscenter.com/develop-true-
emotional-intimacy-between-friends/
Building Peer Relationships https://www.mcgill.ca/connectionslab/files/
connectionslab/peer_relationships_1.pdf
Make new friends and connections
Get a part-time job
Be a foster grandparent https://americorps.gov/serve/fit-finder/
americorps-seniors-foster-grandparent-program
Volunteer
Local Active Aging Centers aka, Senior Centers
AARP Connect to Affect - lots of available resources to avoid isolation
https://connect2affect.org/
MeetUp.com - hosts groups in local towns and cities
AMAVA - online classes for adults https://amava.com/ - or teach a
course

Lifelong Learning - Lifelong learning is the "ongoing, voluntary, and self-motivated" pursuit of knowledge for either personal or professional reasons. Do an online search using the term, "your city and lifelong learning" to find a class or event near you.

OSHA Lifelong Learning - https://www.osherfoundation.org/olli.html

Pet ownership—Owning a pet can reduce the chances of heart disease. It may be that dog owners move more, do more exercise like walking, but pets do play a role in offering social support and connections, and encourages one to stick with a new habit (like walking outdoors.)

Benefits of pet ownership

- Unconditional love
- Sets a routine—help forge discipline and energy management
- Gives social support
- Socializing—an icebreaker between strangers, or as a catalyst for social interaction.
- Boost mental well being—owners are less likely to suffer from depression

    Ask yourself: Can I afford a pet? Am I the only one responsible for the pet? How much time do I have to give one? Will a neighbor or someone else step in to care for the pet if I can't? How much household destruction can I tolerate? What do I hope to gain from having a pet? Do I have the time and resources to properly train a pet? Is my home pet-friendly? Am I now prepared to get one? What are a few things to do to prepare for one? Am I willing to make sacrifices for the pet? Do I have an active travel schedule?

The Power of Pets https://newsinhealth.nih.gov/2018/02/power-pets

Pet Owner Resources https://www.humanesociety.org/resources/pet-owners

More resources for pet owners https://bestfriends.org/advocacy/pet-inclusive-housing/resources-pet-owners

Best Communication Books for Stronger Social Skills https://www.lifehack.org/816339/communication-books

15 Social Skills That Will Make You Successful In Every Aspect Of Life https://www.lifehack.org/articles/communication/15-social-skills-that-will-make-you-successful-every-aspect-life.html

Communication Book https://www.amazon.com/dp/B0762DB43J?tag=s7621-20

SMART SUPPORT COMMUNITY RESOURCES

Neighborly Connections

Build trust, support, and interdependence

Exchange phone numbers and email addresses

Show genuine kindness - "I'm running to the store, need anything?"

"Want to ride with me to Central Market?"

Want to join me for a cup of coffee?

Help each other out by doing simultaneous house watch.

Check in via text with each other to confirm safety.

Expert and Professional Resources

Aging Life Care Professionals works with older clients and families to address their challenges. https://www.aginglifecare.org/

Patient Advocates assist adults with all health related concerns. https://www.aphadvocates.org/directory/

Dietitians for nutrition information. https://www.dietitiancentral.com, https://www.eatright.org

Find a PT directory https://www.apta.org

Find an OT directory https://www.aota.org

Find a Nurse Practitioner https://npfinder.aanp.org

Organizations That Serve Seniors https://srcarecenter.com/article/us-organizations-that-serve-seniors/

2,500+ benefit programs nationwide. Find benefits in your area. https://benefitscheckup.org

Dietetic Associations https://nal.usda.gov/legacy/fnic/dietetic-associations

Support Group Resources

Support Groups https://www.helpguide.org/articles/therapy-medication/support-groups.htm

Find Support Groups https://www.mhanational.org/find-support-groups, https://www.verywellmind.com/find-a-support-group-meeting-near-you-69433

Choose the right support group https://www.mayoclinic.org/healthy-lifestyle/stress-management/in-depth/support-groups/art-20044655 https://peersupportcircles.org/evaluation.htm

Online Caregiver Support Groups https://www.aplaceformom.com/caregiver-resources/articles/caregiver-support-groups

Managing Stress Support Groups https://www.nami.org/Your-Journey/Individuals-with-Mental-Illness/Taking-Care-of-Your-Body/Managing-Stress

Contact local libraries, Area Agency on Aging, and Senior Centers for local support groups

Online Anxiety Support Groups https://www.verywellmind.com/best-online-anxiety-support-groups-4692353

Willingness to Help Resources

Random acts of kindness practice https://ggia.berkeley.edu/practice/random_acts_of_kindness?
_ga=2.79593500.906874614.1640210361-1948293423.1639758735

Writing exercise to foster connection https://ggia.berkeley.edu/practice/
feeling_connected?
_ga=2.72392731.906874614.1640210361-1948293423.1639758735
Loving kindness meditation https://ggia.berkeley.edu/practice/
loving_kindness_meditation?
_ga=2.46778415.906874614.1640210361-1948293423.1639758735
Reminders of connectedness https://ggia.berkeley.edu/practice/
reminders_of_connectedness?
_ga=2.10068925.906874614.1640210361-1948293423.1639758735

SMART PURPOSE RESOURCES
Purpose and Passion
11 Different Views on the Meaning of Life https://
www.theodysseyonline.com/purpose-of-life
Life Purpose https://www.berkeleywellbeing.com/life-purpose.html
Practical Resources to Discover your Purpose in Life https://
youchoosetheway.com/resources-for-purpose-in-life/
Life Purpose Planning https://www.lifepurposeplanning.org/resources/
Taking Charge—Great resource for Life Purpose - an assessment
https://www.takingcharge.csh.umn.edu/what-life-purpose
Best Books on Finding Your Purpose in Life https://
www.developgoodhabits.com/books-purpose/
Smart Moves - how to find your way https://www.smartmoves.life/find-
your-why/
Living Your Purpose http://www.livingyourpurpose.net/
Simple on Purpose https://simpleonpurpose.ca/freebielibrary/
Life Purpose Quiz — draws on decades of experience and research to
help you identify ways you may be preventing yourself from reclaiming
your purpose. https://janlbowen.com/purposequiz/

Greater Good Magazine https://greatergood.berkeley.edu/quizzes/take_quiz/purpose_in_life

SMART FAITH | SPIRITUALITY RESOURCES
Assess Your Spiritual Journey
44 Conversation Questions https://www.evangelismcoach.org/44-conversation-questions/
Spiritual Growth Process
Take the full spiritual assessment https://blog.lifeway.com/growingdisciples/files/2013/08/Spiritual_Growth_Assessment.pdf
Spiritual Growth Assessment https://o.b5z.net/i/u/6053452/f/FBC_Spiritual_Assessment.pdf
Develop Your Spiritual Resources https://www.takingcharge.csh.umn.edu/develop-your-spiritual-resources
Spiritual Resources https://deeperchristian.com/grow-spiritually/
The Spirit Filled Life https://www.cru.org/us/en/train-and-grow/spiritual-growth/the-spirit-filled-life.html

SMART TRANSPORTATION | MOBILITY RESOURCES
Create a Roadmap for Transportation Independence https://eldercare.acl.gov/Public/Resources/Brochures/docs/Give_Up_The_Keys_Roadmap_for_Transportation_Independence.pdf
National Information and Resources https://eldercare.acl.gov/public/resources/topic/Transportation.aspx
Professional driving evaluation and assistance—Directory of driving rehabilitation specialists, American Occupational Therapy Association (AOTA) or the Association for Driver Rehabilitation Specialists (ADED)
National Aging and Disability Transportation Center https://www.nadtc.org/

Alz.org National Transportation Resources https://www.alz.org/media/ Documents/national-senior-transportation-resources.pdf

Easter Seals Transportation https://www.easterseals.com/our-programs/transportation.html

Contact the local Catholic Charity

Directory of driving rehabilitation specialists from the American Occupational Therapy Association (AOTA) or the Association for Driver Rehabilitation Specialists (ADED).

Safe driving tips https://www.arrivealive.mobi/Safe-Driving-in-Heavy-Traffic

Perform an online search using key term, "city or state and transportation resources"

Rideshare apps

Uber is by far the most popular ride sharing service

Lyft, the second-largest ride sharing app by volume

Curb is the #1 taxi app in the US that connects you to fast, convenient and safe rides across the U.S.

Wingz provides transportation to and from airports. Now, they offer around-town rides in a few, select cities. Riders can pick and choose their favorite drivers, and the company promises that moving forward, the service will remain less expensive than a taxi or limo.

Via app uses a "logistics engine" to fill as many seats as possible in cars headed toward popular destinations. Unlike Uber and Lyft, the routes are static—just tell the service where you'd like to go and you'll get dropped off at a nearby location.

Scoop is a ride sharing app for iOS and Android that lets you arrange carpooling with your co-workers and neighbors.

Arro taps into a database of more than 20,000 licensed taxis to provide clients with on-demand transportation. Unfortunately, at this time Arro is only available in a select group of cities, but if you happen to live in New York City, Boston, Miami, and Houston you can take advantage of the services.

BlaBlaCar, BlaBlaCarpool, and bus service are some of the best in recent times. Addressing the problem of rising traffic and gas prices, BlaBlaCar offers a great deal to all of its users. You can pool with other vehicles or passengers covering your common routes. Find a carpool, or if you have a car, you can find people who can travel with you and share expenses.

Waze Carpool is a great app for doing daily travel. Via helps you make the most out of your time and helps you travel faster by getting quick rides to your destination. The app offers an easy to use interface and quick response time.

Karpoolclub app can help you to find your favorite groups to share a ride. A better utilization of your car, van and trusted network to help share your ride for kids, adults, seniors and even pets.

RideConnect.com is a ride sharing platform with which you can create your own rideshare. Develop a ride share program with neighbors, friends, and family.

Transportation Resources

Call your local Area Agency on Aging Department for ride information

Call your city government offices for Paratransit rides

Go to Ridester.com—Uber's program for health rides—Uber Health

Check with your State Health and Human Services Department

Check with your insurance company

Check with your doctor's office and health care provider

You may be eligible for rides via Medicaid to and from your doctor's office, the hospital, and other medical facilities for approved care. Consult your state program for help arranging these services.

Contact Gogograndparent.com

SMART LEGAL MATTERS RESOURCES

American Bar Association is a good resource for legal matters. Their website offers detailed worksheets for health care decision planning. https://www.americanbar.org/groups/law_aging/resources/health_care_decision_making/consumer_s_toolkit_for_health_care_advance_planning/

American Bar Association Free Legal Help https://www.americanbar.org/groups/legal_services/flh-home/flh-free-legal-help/

Legal Aid Assistance https://www.lsc.gov/about-lsc/what-legal-aid/get-legal-help

State Bar List https://generalbar.com/State.aspx

Check with your State Bar Association for Legal (and free) Help

State-based information on Death Certificates, Advance Directives and more https://www.everplans.com/guides/state-by-state-guides

How to be a good health care proxy https://www.everplans.com/articles/how-to-be-a-good-health-care-proxy

Find a Guardian https://www.guardianship.org/find-a-guardian/

Changing Guardians https://www.familylawselfhelpcenter.org/self-help/56-guardianship/additional-orders/194-changing-guardians

A Complete Guide to Legal Guardians https://trustandwill.com/learn/what-is-guardianship

The Ins and Outs of Guardianship and Conservatorship https://www.elderlawanswers.com/guardianship-and-conservatorship-12096

Conservatorship and Guardianship https://www.caregiver.org/resource/conservatorship-and-guardianship/

What You Need to Know about Guardians https://www.naela.org/web/consumers_tab/consumers_library/consumer_brochures/

elder_law_and_special_needs_law_topics/
guardianship_conservatorship.aspx
What Is a Fiduciary, and Why Does It Matter? https://
www.nerdwallet.com/article/investing/
fiduciary#:~:text=A%20fiduciary%20is%20an%20individual,a%20partic
ular%20person%20or%20beneficiary.&text=Working%20with%20a%2
0fiduciary%20financial,not%20all%20advisors%20are%20fiduciaries
Fiduciary 101 https://www.napfa.org/financial-planning/fiduciary-101
Select Legal Forms by State https://www.uslegalforms.com/states/?
gclid=CjwKCAiAxJSPBhAoEiwAeO_fP6QCBPpqhLSuWsvDYeGAjE-
JQmCgVtubG_YiZ-rM396N8tCtSXyQcRoC710QAvD_BwE
End of Life Care Organizations https://www.apa.org/pi/aging/programs/
eol
Death with Dignity Resources https://deathwithdignity.org/resources/
End of life Conversations
https://theconversationproject.org/
https://fivewishes.org/

SMART FUN | ENGAGEMENT RESOURCES
Links for Laughter and Engagement
Jokes Make You Laugh http://www.helpguide.org/life/jokes.htm,
Happiness https://www.helpguide.org/home-pages/well-being-
happiness.htm
Humor Survey: How Well Does Your Sense of Humor Protect You from
Heart Disease University of Maryland Link: http://www.umm.edu/news/
releases/humor_survey.html
Playing Together Creative Play and Lifelong Games http://
www.helpguide.org/life/creative_play_fun_games.htm

Participating in Activities You Enjoy https://www.nia.nih.gov/health/participating-activities-you-enjoy

Over 100 Ways to Play https://www.greatseniorliving.com/articles/fun-activities-for-seniors#games-sports

Hobbies

List of Hobbies List of hobbies https://en.wikipedia.org/wiki/List_of_hobbies

Hobby Help https://hobbyhelp.com/inspiration/list-of-hobbies/

Active Adult Centers

National Institute of Accredited Senior Centers https://www.ncoa.org/article/nisc-nationally-accredited-senior-centers

Public Libraries

Public Libraries in the United States https://librarytechnology.org/libraries/uspublic/

Museums

Best Museums in the USA – Virtual Tour https://joyofmuseums.com/museums/united-states-of-america/

Museums with fine art collections and an online presence http://www.artcyclopedia.com/museums-us.html

List of Art Museums Worldwide https://en.wikipedia.org/wiki/List_of_art_museums

Art Collecting and Gallery Guides

Art Galleries https://art-collecting.com/galleries.htm

World's Top Art Galleries (Listed By Country) https://annarubin.com/art-galleries/

List of most-visited art museums https://en.wikipedia.org/wiki/List_of_most-visited_art_museums

Science Centers

List of Science Centers in the United States https://en.wikipedia.org/ wiki/List_of_science_centers_in_the_United_States

List of Science Centers Worldwide https://en.wikipedia.org/wiki/ List_of_science_museums

Natural History Museums

List of natural History Museums in the United States https:// en.wikipedia.org/wiki/

List_of_natural_history_museums_in_the_United_States

ABOUT THE AUTHOR

Carol Marak, Author, Speaker, Coach, Founder of the Elder Orphan Facebook Group, and former family caregiver. SOLO AND SMART, A Roadmap for a Supportive and Secure Future is based on Carol's retirement plan, the lessons learned from her family caregiving experience. Carol is a native Texan and thrives while living alone in a Dallas urban area. Get in touch with Carol at https://carolmarak.com/index.html or send an email to Carol@CarolMarak.com.

Made in the USA
Las Vegas, NV
22 January 2024

84726953R00118